I0099933

Star Seeker: Your Mission for Galactic Excellence

Excellence for Life

Cj TruHeart

Published by Starfinity Publishing, 2023.

STAR SEEKER: YOUR MISSION FOR GALACTIC EXCELLENCE

First edition. July 27, 2023.

Copyright © 2023 Cj TruHeart.

ISBN: 978-1962165037

Written by Cj TruHeart.

Also by Cj TruHeart

Excellence for Life
Game On: Your Quest for Competitive Excellence
Star Seeker: Your Mission for Galactic Excellence

Watch for more at https://youtube.com/@TruFinity.

Table of Contents

To my Wife, Angel TruHeart, who has been just that, Angelically supportive in all that I've done and continue to do...♥☺

Mission Briefing: Welcome, Star Seeker

《 》

Awakening the Star Seeker

Star Seeker, you stand on the threshold of a transformative voyage, a journey destined to awaken your true potential and ignite the galactic spark within your spirit. Your arrival here is no cosmic accident; instead, it's a celestial convergence, an alignment of your life's experiences that have prepared you for this moment.

Our journey begins here, not on the solid, familiar terrain of the Earth, but in the vast, boundless cosmos that mirrors the untapped expanse of your potential. It's time to step away from the familiar and venture into the star-studded depths of the unknown. Why the cosmos, you may wonder? Because within you resides a universe waiting to be explored, a constellation of dreams, passions, and ambitions that yearn for realization.

As we embark on this expedition, know this: you are a Star Seeker, an explorer of inner realms and outer worlds. And like a star, you are made of the universe's raw elements, shaped by cosmic forces, and guided by the eternal light of your True North Star.

Your journey, Star Seeker, isn't just about reaching a particular destination or achieving a defined objective. It's about the transformation that occurs as you navigate through the cosmos of your own life, exploring your Cosmic Identity and what it truly means to strive for Galactic Excellence.

This book, "Star Seeker: A Mission for Galactic Excellence," is your mission guide, a celestial chart to navigate the cosmos of your mind and soul. It's designed to fuel your journey, equipping you with the insight and tools to terraform the landscape of your very own planet from a choice of billions of stars in the Galaxy, to embrace the stellar potential within you, and to become an architect of your destiny.

So, take a deep breath, feel the anticipation tingle in your veins like the crackling energy of a star about to burst into a supernova. The cosmos is calling and it's time to respond. Welcome, Star Seeker. Your quest for Galactic Excellence begins here. Your universe awaits exploration. Let's awaken the Star Seeker within you.

《 》

The Cosmos Within: Embracing Your Cosmic Identity

We now delve deeper into the cosmos within - your inner universe. This is a realm as vast, as complex, and as breathtakingly beautiful as the star-filled expanses above us. It's a place of infinite possibilities, radiant potential, and celestial mystery, mirroring the cosmos' grandeur. This is your Cosmic Identity.

Your Cosmic Identity is your unique celestial signature, the blend of elements, experiences, dreams, and values that makes you, Star Seeker, truly one-of-a-kind. It is the core of your being, pulsating with the raw energy of a newly born star, teeming with the capacity for Galactic Excellence. And just like the cosmos, your identity isn't static, but rather a dynamic, ever-evolving constellation of experiences and learning.

Embracing this Cosmic Identity means acknowledging your unique place in the universe. It's recognizing that you, too, are made of stardust, composed of the same elements that burn brightly in far-off galaxies. It means understanding that within you lies the potential for greatness that matches the breathtaking spectacle of a star-studded night sky.

To embrace your Cosmic Identity, we must peer into the hidden depths of your universe, exploring the black holes of doubt and uncertainty, the vibrant nebulas of passion and creativity, and the vast voids yearning to be filled with knowledge and experience. This isn't a journey to be rushed, but rather one to be savored, a cosmic exploration filled with awe, wonder, and discovery.

But fear not, Star Seeker. You are not alone on this voyage. As your guide, this book will equip you with the tools and insights needed to navigate your inner cosmos. It will help you to chart a course towards your True North Star, to harness the celestial energies within you, and to shape a planetary corner of the galaxy of your dreams to align with your vision of Galactic Excellence.

So, prepare to embark on this introspective odyssey, to traverse the galaxies of your heart and mind, and to uncover the Cosmic Identity that lies within. Remember, you are not just in the universe, but the universe is within you. You are a unique constellation in this cosmic symphony, and it's time to let your light shine. Embrace your Cosmic Identity, and let's continue our voyage to Galactic Excellence.

《 》

Inner Constellation: Concept of Galactic Excellence

As we journey deeper into your inner cosmos, we encounter an idea of profound significance – Galactic Excellence. Like a supernova illuminating the cosmos with its dazzling light, Galactic Excellence is a radiant vision of achievement that transcends the bounds of earthly success. But what exactly does it entail, and how does it connect to the unique constellation of your Cosmic Identity?

Galactic Excellence isn't simply about accumulating accolades, scaling professional heights, or outrunning your competitors. It isn't tied to any singular achievement, nor is it a measure of your worth in comparison to others. Instead, it is a vision of success that extends far beyond traditional definitions and encompasses a holistic understanding of personal and professional actualization.

To envision Galactic Excellence, think of the cosmos itself. It is expansive, dynamic, and forever evolving. Each celestial body, from the tiniest asteroid to the mightiest galaxy, has a unique path and purpose within the cosmic tapestry. Similarly, your journey to Galactic Excellence is intensely personal, shaped by your unique passions, talents, and aspirations. It's about realizing the potential of your Cosmic Identity, reaching your True North Star, and leaving a meaningful, lasting imprint on the planetary star system of your choice.

Galactic Excellence also extends to how you navigate your journey – the attitude and mindset with which you traverse your inner cosmos. It encourages you to embrace challenges as catalysts for growth, to see failures as black holes leading to new universes of understanding, and to use knowledge as a compass guiding your voyage of self-discovery.

But most importantly, Galactic Excellence is about the constant evolution of your Cosmic Identity. It's about harnessing the energy of your passions, fostering your skills, and continually expanding your understanding of yourself and the world around you. It's about the courage to reach for the stars, to dream beyond earthly limitations, and to create your path in the pursuit of your True North Star.

Embrace this concept, Star Seeker. Adopt it as a guiding principle for your journey through the cosmos. Let it serve as a beacon illuminating your path to personal and professional actualization. This is the essence of your quest - your voyage towards Galactic Excellence.

《 》

The True North Star: Vision for the Future

Star Seeker, as you journey through the vast cosmos of your being amid the intricate constellations of your aspirations and the nebulous clouds of your doubts, one celestial body shines with unwavering radiance – your True North Star. This is your guiding light, a beacon of purpose and ambition that will steer you on your voyage towards Galactic Excellence.

What is this True North Star? It is the embodiment of your deepest dreams and aspirations, the cosmic manifestation of your most profound sense of purpose. It is not a destination fixed in the stellar charts, but a dynamic vision that evolves and shines brighter as you grow and embrace your Cosmic Identity. Your True North Star represents the highest potential of your personal journey for your own defined Galactic Excellence.

Imagine looking up at the cosmos' vast expanse, every star a potential path. Among these infinite pathways, there exists one that resonates with you at a profound level, a stellar trajectory that calls out to the explorer in you inviting you to embark on a journey like no other. This path leads you to defining your True North Star.

Your True North Star isn't defined by societal expectations, nor does it mirror someone else's journey. It's uniquely yours, reflective of your passions, talents, and values. It's the vision of a future where you achieve your own version of success – Galactic Excellence. How do you define your own version of success? How do you create your journey to achieve your North Star?

As we traverse the cosmos within, this star will serve as our guiding light, illuminating our way forward, helping us chart the course of our voyage. It will guide us when we traverse the black holes of doubt, providing a sense of direction when we feel lost in the vast expanse of the cosmos. It's the shining light we will strive to reach, always there, always leading us forward on our journey.

So, Star Seeker, take a moment to gaze upon the cosmos within. Look for that bright, unwavering star that calls out to you. Listen to its cosmic whisper, urging you to follow. This is your True North Star, your beacon towards Galactic Excellence.

⟨ ⟩

Navigating Inner and Outer Space

As we prepare to journey towards your True North Star, we must equip ourselves with a holistic understanding of our cosmic course. Our voyage isn't confined to the boundaries of your inner cosmos, the realm of introspection and self-realization. It also extends into the outer space, the external world of interactions, relationships, and societal structures. Understanding this duality and the interplay between these realms is a crucial part of our mission, Star Seeker.

Imagine two celestial bodies orbiting each other, their paths influenced by each other's gravity. In the same way, your inner and outer spaces exist in a delicate dance of mutual influence. Your thoughts, beliefs, and values (inner space) shape how you interact with your environment, while the external world, in turn, influences your inner state.

In your journey towards Galactic Excellence, you'll traverse the galaxies of self-awareness and self-belief, as well as navigate the outer realms of societal expectations and shared realities. One moment you may be diving into the depths of your inner space, exploring your strengths, weaknesses, fears, and dreams. The next, you might be soaring through the external world, learning to interact effectively with others, and striving to create a positive impact.

But how do you navigate this intricate dance of inner and outer space? How do you plot your course through this complex celestial choreography? Enter the concept of Galactic Colonization - a space explorers guide to your unique framework for navigating your journey towards Galactic Excellence.

Space exploration with the idea for Galactic Colonization requires a constellation of values, strategies, and actions that guide you as you navigate your inner and outer spaces. It's your compass in this dual-universe, your celestial chart to steer you on your journey. It's a system that helps you align your internal world with your external actions, ensuring that you stay true to your Cosmic Identity as you strive for your True North Star.

Within your chosen settled Star System, each planet represents an aspect of your life - career, relationships, health, hobbies, personal growth - all orbiting around the radiant sun of your True North Star. The goal is to align these planets in harmony, setting them on a path that leads towards Excellence.

Star Seeker, as we delve into the chapters ahead, we will explore your chosen Star System's creation and fine-tuning. We will learn how to harmonize the inner and outer space dance and ensure they orbit cohesively towards your vision of success. The cosmos awaits us. It's time to navigate our journey, and set course for the stars.

《 》

Facing the Black Holes: Embracing Challenges

We must acknowledge that our journey won't always be a tranquil voyage through starlit spaces. We will encounter celestial anomalies and challenging aspects of our exploration – the black holes. These represent our fears, challenges, and uncertainties, the adversities we must face on our quest towards excellence.

Black holes, in their mysterious allure, often provoke a sense of fear and uncertainty. They seem to swallow all light and hope, offering nothing but darkness in return. However, within this book, we perceive these black holes differently. Instead of seeing them as insurmountable obstacles, we perceive them as opportunities for growth, transformation, and discovery.

Every challenge you encounter, every fear that creeps into your mind, and every uncertainty that clouds your vision is a black hole that you have the potential to navigate. In overcoming these challenges, you become stronger, more resilient, and better equipped for your cosmic journey.

The goal of this book is to provide you with the astrolabe of resilience, the spaceship of courage, and the navigational system of wisdom. These tools will empower you to face these black holes, to understand their nature, and to transform their energy into fuel for your journey.

We'll learn how to harness the hidden power of adversity, how to turn the gravity of challenges into slingshots that propel us forward. We'll face our fears, dive into our doubts, and emerge from the other side with newfound strength and understanding.

Remember, every black hole navigated brings us closer to our True North Star. It's through facing these challenges that we grow and expand, that we refine our course and sharpen our resolve. With this book as your guide, you'll learn to embrace the black holes in your journey, seeing them not as threats, but as unique opportunities for growth and self-discovery. So, fear not the challenges that lie ahead. For within the heart of every black hole, lies a universe of potential waiting to be discovered.

〈 〉

Stardust Collective: The Power of Connection

As we set course for our True North Star, it's easy to assume that our journey towards Galactic Excellence is a solitary one. After all, it's our unique Cosmic Identity at the helm, our individual Solar Star System guiding our route. However, Star Seeker, let me assure you, our voyage through the cosmos need not be a lonely one.

In the vastness of the universe, stars often form clusters, drawing together in mutual gravitation, their paths intertwined in a celestial ballet. Similarly, in our journey towards Galactic Excellence, we are not isolated entities drifting in space but part of a grand constellation of Star Seekers. We are, in essence, part of a collective, a community of explorers each charting their unique course towards their True North Star.

Why is this connection important? Because we are inherently social beings, we thrive on shared insights, collective growth, and mutual support. Our journey towards Galactic Excellence becomes more enriching when we interact with fellow Star Seekers. When we share our insights and learn from theirs, when we support each other in navigating our respective black holes, we evolve and grow together.

This book serves not only as a navigational chart but also as a communication device, a cosmic relay that bridges the distances between Star Seekers. It's an invitation to engage, to connect, to learn from and support each other. Remember, as you move forward on your journey, you're not just charting a course for yourself. You're also lighting the way for others, just as they illuminate your path with their unique insights and experiences.

In the chapters that follow, you will find opportunities to engage with fellow Star Seekers, to share your insights and learn from theirs. You'll learn the importance of connection and how to harness the power of collective wisdom on your journey towards Galactic Excellence.

So, let's set course, Star Seeker. As we journey towards our True North Star, let's do so with the knowledge that we are not alone. We are part of a grand constellation of explorers each on our unique voyage of discovery and growth. Together, we'll light up the cosmos, one Star Seeker at a time.

《 》

L ift-Off: Beginning Your Journey

Star Seeker, the countdown has ended. We've charted our course, explored the cosmos within and without, and prepared ourselves for the inevitable black holes. We've recognized the power of connection and understood that our voyage is not solitary but shared. Our spaceship of courage and curiosity is fueled and ready. Now, it's time for liftoff, time to set sail towards your defined Galactic Excellence.

This is a significant moment, a pivotal point in time where we leave the confines of our current reality and embark on an exhilarating journey of discovery and growth. This journey, Star Seeker, isn't about reaching a fixed destination but about the pursuit, the exploration, and the continual transformation that comes with navigating towards your True North Star.

There will be moments of self-doubt, of fear, of uncertainty. Remember, these feelings are natural. They are part of the process, part of the cosmic dance. Embrace them. Allow them to fuel your determination, to sharpen your resilience, to deepen your understanding. These are not setbacks but stepping stones on your path to Galactic Excellence.

There will also be moments of triumph, of joy, of illumination. Cherish these moments. Let them remind you of the power within you, the infinite potential of your Cosmic Identity. Let them illuminate your path, infuse your journey with purpose and inspire your continued voyage.

This is your journey, Star Seeker, one that's as unique as the celestial signature you carry within. No two paths to Galactic Excellence are the same and that's the beauty of this journey. It's an expedition that takes us beyond the ordinary, beyond our comfort zones and into the realm of extraordinary possibilities.

Harness your courage, stoke your curiosity, and get ready to journey towards your True North Star. Every chapter of this book will serve as a navigational guide, a celestial beacon lighting your path towards Galactic Excellence.

So, **Star Seeker**, are you ready? It's time for lift-off. It's time to navigate the cosmos, to explore the extraordinary and to embrace the beauty of the journey. Galactic Excellence awaits. Let's begin our voyage towards the stars.

Chapter 1: The Gravity Well of Perspective

The Cosmic Power of Mindset

Greetings, Star Seeker! As we commence our grand journey towards Galactic Excellence, the first stop on our interstellar map is understanding the pivotal role of mindset. Just like how the course of celestial bodies is influenced by the gravity wells in the cosmos, our lives are influenced significantly by our mindset, an invisible yet powerful force that shapes our existence and journey. It's a gravity well of perspective, if you will.

Our mindset is an intricate framework of beliefs, attitudes, and perceptions that guide our thoughts, actions, and responses to situations. Like a starship's autopilot, it often operates beneath our conscious awareness, steering us without our explicit direction. We might not always realize it, but our mindset forms the very core of our Cosmic Identity. It's the foundation for our space exploration and the compass that guides us towards our True North Star.

How we perceive ourselves, others, and the world around us; how we approach challenges and setbacks; how we define and strive for success – it all hinges on our mindset. A positive mindset, like a friendly gravity well, pulls us into a trajectory of growth, fulfillment, and Galactic Excellence. Conversely, a negative mindset, akin to a black hole, can pull us away from our desired path, forcing us into a downward spiral of self-doubt and stagnation.

As Star Seekers, it is incumbent upon us to recognize the enormous power our mindset wields and learn to harness this power for our journey. It's not about tricking ourselves into relentless positivity or denying the realities of life. It's about cultivating a mindset that serves us, a mindset that transforms obstacles into opportunities, fears into fuel, and dreams into reality.

This chapter, Star Seeker, invites you to examine your gravity well of perspective – to explore its depths, understand its pull, and learn to navigate its force.

⟪ ⟫

Understanding Gravity Wells

In our grand cosmos, gravity is the invisible force that orders the universe. It pulls celestial bodies into orbit, keeps planets in check, and forms the cosmic ballet of galaxies dancing across the cosmos. At the heart of this dance are 'Gravity Wells' - regions of space where gravity is so strong that it warps the very fabric of space-time.

These wells pull objects towards their center, influencing their trajectory and speed.

Now, imagine your mindset as a sort of gravity well, an invisible force exerting a significant influence on your life's trajectory. Each thought, each belief, each attitude within your mindset has its own gravitational pull. Positive thoughts pull you toward success, fulfillment, and excellence. Whereas negative thoughts can pull you into self-doubt, fear, and stagnation. Like a spaceship navigating through the cosmos, the course of your life is continuously affected by the pull of these mental gravity wells.

The beauty of this cosmic metaphor is in its profound implications. In space, the key to escaping a gravity well isn't fighting against it but leveraging its pull to propel forward. Similarly, we don't have to wage war against our mindset; we need to understand it, navigate it, and use its pull to our advantage.

Are you starting to see the power your mindset holds, Star Seeker? Like the unseen force that directs the cosmos, your mindset guides the path of your life. But remember, you are not merely a spaceship adrift. You are the commander, the astronaut at the helm, capable of adjusting your course and navigating your gravity well of perspective towards your True North Star. The question is, how do we cultivate a mindset, a gravity well, that serves our mission of Galactic Excellence? Let's explore further.

《 》

The Pull of a Positive Mindset

Picture a celestial body with a positive gravitational pull. Its strength gently guides other celestial bodies into a harmonious dance around it, creating a celestial tapestry of movement, order, and beauty. This is the metaphorical equivalent of a positive mindset. A positive mindset serves as a gravity well that can pull you towards a life filled with fulfillment, success, and joy.

A positive mindset isn't about plastering a smile on our faces at all times or pretending everything is fine when it's not. Rather, it is about understanding that we have the power to choose our responses to the events of our lives. It's about embracing growth, seeking solutions, expressing gratitude, cultivating optimism, and fostering resilience. It's the ability to find silver linings in the darkest of black holes and see challenges as opportunities for growth and discovery.

This perspective is deeply rooted in the principles of positive psychology, a branch of psychology that focuses on personal growth rather than pathology. It champions the idea that happiness and fulfillment come from highlighting and harnessing one's strengths rather than merely fixing what's wrong.

By applying these principles, you can start to reshape your gravity well of perspective. By consciously choosing to respond positively to life's challenges, you begin to shape a mindset that draws you towards your goals, towards your True North Star. You start to create a gravity well that is conducive to your journey of Galactic Excellence.

Remember, positivity doesn't mean denying hardships or difficulties. The cosmos is filled with black holes, supernovas, and all kinds of cosmic phenomena that could wreak havoc on a journeying spaceship. But equipped with the right tools and perspective, you can use these cosmic events as stepping stones rather than stumbling blocks.

Like an expert astronaut navigating through the cosmos, mastering the power of a positive mindset is key to your voyage. As you begin to understand and apply this, you become capable of turning the gravity well's pull into a propelling force towards your vision of Galactic Excellence. So, strap in, Star Seeker, as we delve into understanding the gravity well's polar opposite – the black hole of a negative mindset.

《 》

The Danger of a Negative Mindset

Now, picture the ominous black hole, a region of spacetime exhibiting such powerful gravitational pull that nothing, not even light, can escape from it. It's a voracious cosmic entity that devours everything within its reach. Let's equate this black hole to a negative mindset. Just like the black hole's irresistible pull, a negative mindset can trap us in a destructive pattern of thinking, drawing us away from our True North Star and towards a reality far removed from our vision of Galactic Excellence.

Negative thinking often manifests in forms such as self-doubt, fear of failure, anxiety, pessimism, and chronic dissatisfaction. Like the black hole's event horizon, once we fall into this pattern, it can feel almost impossible to escape. Negative thoughts become a self-fulfilling prophecy, distorting our reality and obscuring our potential.

The damage isn't merely philosophical; it's profoundly practical. Studies consistently link a persistent negative mindset with poor health outcomes, reduced lifespan, relationship issues, career stagnation, and diminished life satisfaction. However, Star Seeker, do not despair. Just as the universe has methods to counter black holes, we too have strategies to manage our negative mindset.

The first step to escape this black hole is recognizing its existence. Awareness of your thought patterns gives you a fighting chance against being drawn into negativity. Listen to the words you tell yourself. Do they serve your mission or hinder it? When you become aware of a negative thought, try not to judge or resist it. Instead, acknowledge it and gently redirect your focus towards something more positive or productive.

Cognitive restructuring, a popular tool in cognitive-behavioral therapy, can be of immense help. It involves identifying and challenging irrational or negative thoughts and systematically replacing them with more accurate and beneficial ones. Mindfulness and meditation are also powerful tools that can help you maintain a more positive and present mindset.

Remember, Star Seeker, a journey towards Galactic Excellence isn't about never encountering black holes; it's about learning to navigate around them. It's about understanding their nature, recognizing their pull, and adjusting your course to ensure you remain headed towards your True North Star. Yes, the pull of a black hole can be strong, but remember, you are the commander of your voyage. With the right mindset, you possess the strength to chart your course and determine your destiny. The next section of our journey will provide you with a toolbox of strategies to manage your mindset's gravitational pull effectively. So, let's warp forward!

⟨ ⟩

E scaping the Gravity Well: Shifting Mindsets

Imagine, Star Seeker, being pulled towards a black hole. This pull may seem inescapable, but with the right strategies and navigation tools, it is indeed possible to break free from its oppressive force. Just like this, negative mindsets, though seemingly relentless, can be transformed with the right tools. Consider this section your navigational toolkit, aimed at guiding you towards the radiant luminosity of a positive mindset and away from the dark pull of negativity.

The first tool in your arsenal is mindfulness. When we're lost in the cosmos of our thoughts, we often find ourselves ruminating about the past or worrying about the future. Mindfulness is the act of anchoring ourselves in the present moment. Just like an astronaut tethered to their spacecraft, mindfulness ensures we don't drift aimlessly in the depths of negativity. By grounding ourselves in the now, we can observe our thoughts objectively, allowing us to notice any negative patterns without being swept away in them.

Next, we have cognitive restructuring. Think of it as a skilled engineer who can rebuild a spaceship's faulty engine. In cognitive restructuring, we identify, challenge, and alter our negative thought patterns. We start by catching our pessimistic thoughts in action, challenging their validity and then swapping them with more positive, accurate statements. For instance, if you catch yourself thinking, "I will never achieve Galactic Excellence," challenge this thought. Is it really true? More likely, it's just fear talking. Replace it with, "With determination and effort, I can achieve Galactic Excellence."

Lastly, we introduce the growth mindset. This approach is the belief that our abilities and intelligence can be developed through dedication and hard work. In essence, a growth mindset sees potential for improvement, even in failure. To cultivate a growth mindset, start seeing challenges as opportunities for growth rather than threats. When you stumble, instead of thinking, "I am a failure," remind yourself, "I am learning and growing."

It's important to remember, Star Seeker, that shifting your mindset isn't about ignoring the realities of life. Challenges and setbacks will inevitably arise during our voyage through the cosmos. However, by changing our mindset, we can alter our reactions to these challenges. The gravity well of a negative mindset might seem daunting, but remember, just as spacecraft use gravitational slingshots to propel themselves into deep space, we too can use the gravity of our mindsets to thrust ourselves towards Galactic Excellence.

Hold on tight. With these tools at your disposal, you're now ready to venture deeper into your self-defined cosmic journey. The galaxies of potential are within your reach. It's time to blast off into the boundless cosmos of Galactic Excellence!

《 》

Applying Cosmic Shifts to Everyday Life

Much like the practicalities of space travel, navigating the galaxies of our lives requires a certain level of grounding. Thus far, we've discussed the theory behind escaping the gravity well of perspective. Now, let's translate these cosmic concepts into the everyday orbits of our lives.

To begin, let's consider mindfulness. Picture a small satellite orbiting around a busy planet, taking in all that is happening below. This satellite represents your mindful self, calmly observing the comings and goings of thoughts and emotions without judgement. Here's a simple exercise to try: Set aside five minutes each day to do nothing but breathe and observe your thoughts. Watch them as the satellite watches the bustling planet below. Acknowledge their presence but refrain from diving into their narrative. This is the essence of mindfulness – a non-judgmental observation of the present.

Now, let's talk about cognitive restructuring. Imagine your mind as a bustling spaceport, with thoughts taking off and landing at a rapid pace. The key here is to keep the air traffic under control, ensuring the negative thoughts aren't dominating the skies. Keep a thought journal, logging any negative thoughts that touch down throughout the day. At the end of each day, revisit these thoughts. Challenge their validity and reconstruct them with a more positive frame. Turn, "I made a huge mistake at work, I'm useless" into "I made a mistake at work, but everyone makes mistakes, and I can learn from this."

Lastly, cultivating a growth mindset is like charting a new course for an unexplored galaxy. It's uncharted territory that requires courage and resilience. One practical way to develop a growth mindset is through the 'yet' strategy. Whenever you find yourself thinking, "I can't do this," simply add the word 'yet' at the end. It's a small word, but it possesses immense power, reminding us that we are always on a journey of growth and learning.

Each of these exercises can be likened to conducting routine system checks on your spaceship, ensuring you're on course and ready for the voyage ahead. Keep in mind, these are not one-time activities, but practices to be cultivated and maintained as we continue our journey.

Remember, Star Seeker, the gravity well of your perspective is immensely powerful. When harnessed correctly, it can slingshot you towards your True North Star with incredible speed. As we embark on this mission for Galactic Excellence, let us regularly check our cosmic compass, fine-tuning our mindset and optimizing our trajectory. The stars are within your reach, fellow voyager. Continue to navigate your journey with courage and anticipation, for the cosmos awaits your unique touch.

《 》

Embrace Your Gravity Well

As we conclude this chapter, let's hover for a moment, just like a spacecraft on the edge of a gravity well, caught in a delicate dance between the gravitational pull of the celestial body below and the beckoning vastness of the cosmos beyond. This dance, this balancing act, is akin to the journey we're on, Star Seeker. The gravity well of our mindset can either pull us down into a black hole of doubt, fear, and self-limitation or propel us forward, flinging us into the limitless expanse of our untapped potential.

Like seasoned astronauts adapting to the effects of gravity, we must learn to adjust and align ourselves with the powerful forces within us. Our mindset, represented by the gravity well, is not a fixed entity. It is mutable, changeable, and under our command. It's about understanding that we have the capacity to wield its power to our advantage.

Your journey towards Galactic Excellence will require courage, resilience, and a mindset willing to explore uncharted territories. Yet, it is not an impossible task. Quite the contrary, Star Seeker! By recognizing the profound power of your own perspective, by understanding its gravity well and learning how to navigate its pull, you are already on your way to reaching your True North Star.

It's time now to fasten your seat belts and engage your spaceship's thrusters. Embrace the gravity well of your perspective, harness its pull, and use it to slingshot your way to the cosmic heights of your ambitions. Don't fear its weight, but instead, use it to build momentum, fueling your course and directing your trajectory towards Galactic Excellence.

Chapter 2: Preparing for Lift-Off - Charting Your Cosmic Course

The Importance of Charting Your Course

Welcome, Star Seeker, to the launchpad of your journey towards Galactic Excellence. We understand that our voyage won't be aimless, nor will it be a simple straight-line course. The stars, planets, and galaxies are strewn across the canvas of space, creating an intricate, beautiful pattern that, at first glance, may appear overwhelming. The key to successfully navigate this celestial maze is charting a clear, specific course – your Cosmic Course.

Much like early explorers charted their routes using the constellations, we too will plot our course across the universe. Our map? A set of clear and specific goals – bright beacons in the interstellar void that will guide us on our journey. Our compass? A deep understanding of who we are, what we desire, and the direction we wish to travel.

Goalsetting is as essential to our journey as a navigation system is to a spacecraft. A space vessel equipped with the most advanced technology but lacking a destination would aimlessly drift in space, a fate we seek to avoid. Clear, ambitious goals will fuel our journey, providing us with the motivation, direction, and purpose needed to transcend the limits of our current reality and reach for the stars.

By setting goals, we are not merely declaring our desired destination; we are committing to the journey, to the hardships and joys it may entail, and to ourselves. It is the first, vital step in transforming our dreams into reality. It is, Star Seeker, how we prepare for lift-off.

《 》

The Star Map: Defining Your True North Star

In our journey through the cosmos, Star Seeker, each of us has a shining beacon that lights our way. This beacon, your True North Star, is the ultimate destination, the vision that encapsulates what Galactic Excellence means for you. It is the point on your celestial map where all your trajectories converge, guiding you in the endless cosmos.

Defining your True North Star is not a task to be taken lightly. It represents your ultimate ambitions, your highest aspirations. It is a reflection of your deepest values and the future you wish to create. This is not a mere goal, but a vision that gives purpose and meaning to your journey. It is the galactic embodiment of your heart's deepest desires.

Visualize your True North Star as a beacon of brilliant light in the depth of space, a beacon that is distinctly yours. What does it represent for you? Is it a particular achievement, a state of being, or a contribution to the world? Remember, there are no right or wrong answers - only what resonates deeply within your Cosmic Identity.

Begin by looking inward. Reflect upon your values, passions, and skills. Contemplate your ideal future. Ask yourself: "In my quest for Galactic Excellence, what am I ultimately striving for?" Keep in mind that your True North Star should be ambitious yet achievable. It should inspire you, instilling a sense of purpose that will drive you forward even amid the most challenging cosmic storms.

Take your time with this, Star Seeker. Defining your True North Star is a process of deep introspection. It's okay if your star seems a bit blurry at first; clarity often comes with time and introspection. Remember, this celestial journey is not a race, but a voyage of discovery, growth, and transformation. With your True North Star in sight, the trajectory of your journey will become clearer, guiding you towards your vision of Galactic Excellence.

《 》

Short-Term Pulsars: Setting S.M.A.R.T. Goals

With your True North Star identified, it's time to chart the course. Yet, the vast expanse of the cosmos between you and your ultimate destination might seem overwhelming. Fear not, Star Seeker, for we navigate these vast cosmic distances step by step, or more aptly, star by star. In this context, our guiding lights will be the pulsars, rapidly spinning neutron stars that emit beams of radiation — analogous to the short-term goals that illuminate our path towards the True North Star.

Setting these short-term goals, our pulsars, brings the lofty vision of the True North Star within reach. They break down our grand quest into manageable sections, helping us maintain momentum and offering chances to celebrate progress along the way. For these pulsars to effectively guide us, they need to be S.M.A.R.T. - Specific, Measurable, Achievable, Relevant, and Time-bound.

Specific goals are well-defined and clear. They answer questions like: What do I want to accomplish? Why is this goal important? What resources or limits are involved?

Measurable goals can be tracked and assessed allowing you to gauge progress and adjust your course if necessary. Consider how you'll know when you've reached your goal. What evidence will show that you're advancing towards your True North Star?

Achievable goals, while challenging, are within your capabilities. These goals encourage growth without causing undue stress or setting you up for disappointment.

Relevant goals align with your larger vision, your True North Star. They should resonate with your values and long-term objectives, maintaining your motivation and focus.

Time-bound goals have a clear timeframe, which creates a sense of urgency and prompts action. Deadlines can vary from days to months or even years, depending on the nature of the goal.

As you chart your cosmic course, fill your star map with these pulsars, your S.M.A.R.T. goals. Each one is a step forward, a beacon of accomplishment lighting your way to Galactic Excellence. Remember, the journey to your True North Star is not a straight line, and that's perfectly okay. As you grow and evolve, so too might your goals. Be flexible, Star Seeker, and allow your journey through the cosmos to be a dance rather than a march. Your Galactic Excellence awaits!

⟪ ⟫

Quantum Leaps and Small Steps: Balancing Ambition and Reality

As Star Seekers, our journey towards Galactic Excellence calls us to the edges of the cosmos where Quantum Leaps of progress feel both tantalizing and terrifying. They represent our ambitious, long-term goals, the dream destinations we aspire to reach on our star maps. They encapsulate the significant changes we wish to manifest in our lives – perhaps a profound career shift, a life-altering personal transformation, or the realization of a lifelong dream.

Yet, Quantum Leaps can't be achieved in one giant stride. The reality of our cosmic journey is such that these grand aspirations are reached through a series of smaller steps. Like the delicate dance of electrons jumping between energy levels within an atom, we too must appreciate the power of Small Steps.

Small Steps are achievable, short-term goals that serve as stepping stones to the larger Quantum Leaps. They carry us from one pulsar to the next, ensuring that we make constant progress towards our True North Star. These Small Steps allow us to build skills, gain confidence, and gather the momentum needed for the more significant jumps. They're the heartbeats of our journey, each one an affirmation that we are making progress, that we are becoming the Star Seekers we aspire to be.

Balancing Quantum Leaps and Small Steps is a crucial aspect of charting our cosmic course. While Quantum Leaps keep us anchored to our dreams and ambitions, Small Steps ensure that we remain grounded in reality, providing a pragmatic route towards our larger goals. Neither is more important than the other, and both are necessary to achieve Galactic Excellence. As you navigate your journey, remember: even the smallest step can lead to a Quantum Leap in the right direction. Embrace the dance of ambition and reality, and let it propel you towards your True North Star.

《 》

Navigational Adjustments: Embracing Change and Flexibility

As we embark on our cosmic journey, our star map in hand, we are often met with the vast and profound realization that space is not static. Stars shimmer and shift, galaxies revolve, and celestial bodies are in a constant dance of movement and change. In the same way, our voyage towards Galactic Excellence is not linear; it ebbs and flows, expands and contracts.

Our initial course, charted with meticulous precision, may become clouded by nebulae of uncertainty or affected by the gravitational pull of life's unforeseen events. A career transition, a personal crisis, a worldwide pandemic, or simply a change of heart, can throw us off our original course. It's important to acknowledge that these shifts are not anomalies or signs of failure, but inherent aspects of our cosmic journey.

The key to thriving amidst these changes lies in our ability to make navigational adjustments - a commitment to embracing change and flexibility. Our star map should not be a rigid route set in stone but a living guide that evolves with us. We need to learn to trust our intuition, read the cosmic signs, and adjust our trajectory as needed.

Whether we're fine-tuning our approach to a goal, or shifting our True North Star entirely, embracing change is a vital part of charting our cosmic course. It requires courage to let go of outdated plans and adopt new ones that better serve our journey.

But remember, Star Seeker, the universe favors the flexible. Each adjustment we make, each change we embrace, brings us closer to our unique path of Galactic Excellence. Let's harness the power of change and flexibility, knowing that our capacity to adapt is one of our greatest tools in this mission.

《 》

Mapping the Intergalactic Terrain: Preparing for Challenges

Just as the grand cosmos is filled with breathtaking constellations and awe-inspiring galaxies, it also holds its share of formidable black holes and meteor showers - unforeseen challenges that may loom in our path to Galactic Excellence. The first step in navigating these hurdles is acknowledging their existence. They are an intrinsic part of the intergalactic terrain that shapes our cosmic journey, and thus, understanding them becomes essential.

As we embark on this remarkable journey, we must prepare ourselves for encounters with such cosmic adversities. They may come in the form of self-doubt, fear of failure, or external setbacks. But remember, like comets streaking across the sky, these trials hold within them an opportunity for learning and growth.

Being prepared for these challenges doesn't mean we need to live in perpetual fear or anxiety. Instead, it's about equipping ourselves with the tools and resilience to navigate through them. It's about creating a reliable spaceship of coping strategies, emotional support systems, and self-care routines. It's about cultivating an unshakeable belief in ourselves and our ability to adapt and overcome.

We need to visualize these challenges as black holes that threaten to pull us off course, but also as potential gateways to new dimensions of self-discovery and learning. By acknowledging and preparing for these cosmic trials, we transform them from insurmountable obstacles into springboards for personal growth.

In the face of adversity, remember the power of your Cosmic Identity and the pull of your True North Star. Let's map out the intergalactic terrain, embracing the beautiful and the formidable, and prepare ourselves to navigate this epic voyage to Galactic Excellence. Together, we can convert these challenges into our allies and move forward with unwavering determination and courage.

《 》

Fueling Up for Lift-Off

As we stand at the threshold of our cosmic journey, looking up at the twinkling expanse of possibilities stretching above us, we are filled with a sense of wonder, anticipation, and, yes, perhaps a little apprehension. That is not only okay, but it's a testament to the incredible journey we are about to undertake, the daring leap we are preparing to make into the uncharted territories of our highest potential.

Throughout this chapter, we have charted our course, defined our True North Star, and set our sights on the Pulsars that will guide us. We've grappled with the balance between Quantum Leaps and Small Steps and learned to embrace the fluid dance of change and flexibility. And we've peered into the potential black holes that lie ahead, not with fear, but with preparedness, resilience, and a commitment to navigate them with grace.

This process of exploration, self-reflection, and planning is our initial fueling phase - it's what powers our engines for the lift-off into the expansive universe of Galactic Excellence. It is as much an adventure as the journey itself, filled with moments of discovery, self-insight, and growth.

We are embarking on this quest not just with the aim of reaching our True North Star, but to transform ourselves in the process, to be molded by the cosmos into beings of Galactic Excellence. Each of us stands at the helm of our own spaceship, with the universe spread out before us. It is time to trust in our preparations, ignite our engines, and prepare for lift-off!

Chapter 3: Dark Energy – The Hidden Force of Emotional Intelligence

U nmasking the Dark Energy

Just as you wouldn't embark on an intergalactic expedition without a detailed map of the cosmos, you can't navigate your journey towards Galactic Excellence without comprehending the deep universe within you. Like the elusive Dark Energy—unseen yet omnipresent, silent yet incredibly powerful—there lies a hidden force within us all that holds the power to shape our cosmic voyage. This force is Emotional Intelligence.

It is said that Dark Energy makes up about 68% of the universe. Despite being invisible and mysterious, it's the leading player in the grand cosmic dance, causing galaxies to rush away from each other at increasing speeds. Similarly, Emotional Intelligence, though often overlooked, forms the essential fabric of our experiences and interactions, giving momentum to our life's endeavors.

This chapter will guide you in understanding your emotional universe, akin to charting the dark expanses of interstellar space. You will learn to reveal your inner Dark Energy—your Emotional Intelligence—and harness it as a propelling force in your cosmic quest. As we venture into the heart of this exciting journey, let's begin by exploring the complex interplay of rationality and emotion, two seemingly contrasting elements that come together to form the backbone of Emotional Intelligence. Welcome to the voyage within, Star Seeker.

⟨ ⟩

The Quantum Quandary: Rationality vs Emotion

Now that we've set our sights on the Dark Energy within us, it's time to delve deeper into the cosmos of our mind. Picture it as a binary star system—two stars, rationality and emotion, constantly orbiting each other. At times, they seem to be in stark opposition, like celestial bodies on opposing trajectories. However, their relationship is not a collision course but a cosmic dance, an intricate interplay of gravity and momentum. This dance underpins your emotional intelligence.

The Quantum Quandary that many of us face is this: Should we follow our heart or our head? It's a question as old as consciousness itself, echoing across the millennia. The popular narrative often posits these two forces as antagonists in an epic celestial duel. But just as particles in the quantum realm can exist in multiple states at once, so can our rationality and emotions coexist and cooperate within us.

Imagine rationality as the pulsar, a rotating neutron star that emits a steady beam of electromagnetic radiation—precise, predictable, and unerring. In contrast, emotions could be likened to a red giant, expansive and powerful, radiating warmth and energy in all directions. When the pulsar's focused intensity integrates with the red giant's encompassing passion, they form a binary system—a beacon of light piercing through the vastness of the cosmos.

In the realm of Emotional Intelligence, rationality and emotion are not rivals but allies. It is about balancing the analytical with the empathetic, integrating the logical mind with the passionate heart. When these seemingly contrasting forces unite, they create a robust framework for decision-making, problem-solving, and interpersonal relationships.

Just like the vast cosmos with all its contrasts and paradoxes, our mind thrives on this balance. Engaging both rationality and emotion, comprehending their roles, and fostering their synergy—these are essential skills for every Star Seeker. In this journey towards Galactic Excellence, **remember**: your mind is not a battleground of opposing forces but a fertile ground for cooperation and growth. Harnessing this harmony is the key to unlocking the potent force of your Emotional Intelligence.

As we embark further on this journey, let's turn our attention to the core components of Emotional Intelligence and how to cultivate them. Strap in, Star Seeker—the adventure continues.

⟨ ⟩

The Four Pillars of Emotional Intelligence

Let us now voyage deeper into the cosmic expanse of emotional intelligence, venturing towards its Four Pillars. Much like the fundamental forces that govern the universe - gravity, electromagnetism, the strong nuclear force, and the weak nuclear force - these Pillars guide the course of our emotional universe. Together, they create the framework of emotional intelligence: self-awareness, self-management, social awareness, and relationship management.

Self-Awareness: The Personal Pulsar

The first Pillar, Self-Awareness, is your Personal Pulsar. It serves as the navigational beacon, a celestial lighthouse guiding your journey into the soul. It is about recognizing your emotions as they occur, understanding your strengths and weaknesses, and deciphering your needs and desires. By shining its unwavering light on your inner universe, Self-Awareness helps you comprehend the impact of your feelings on your actions and decisions.

Self-Management: The Orbital Resilience

The second Pillar, Self-Management, reflects Orbital Resilience. Just as celestial bodies maintain their orbits amidst cosmic turbulence, effective self-management helps you maintain balance amidst emotional upheavals. It involves managing your emotions in a healthy way, taking initiative, following through on commitments, and adapting to changing circumstances without spiraling into a black hole of confusion or despair.

Social Awareness: The Galactic Empathy

The third Pillar, Social Awareness, expands our perspective to Galactic Empathy. This realm is not confined to the introspective journey within, but it ventures outwards into the cosmic sea of social interactions. It involves recognizing and understanding the emotions and perspectives of others, just as a telescope discerns distant stars and galaxies. It's the ability to pick up on emotional cues, understand group dynamics, and appreciate the cultural and social diversity within your cosmic voyage.

Relationship Management: The Interstellar Diplomacy

The fourth and final Pillar, Relationship Management, relates to Interstellar Diplomacy. It takes insight and understanding from the other three Pillars and applies them to manage your relationships effectively. Like a seasoned diplomat fostering peaceful interstellar relations, this skill involves clear communication, managing conflicts, inspiring others, and cultivating meaningful and beneficial relationships.

As we navigate through these four Pillars of Emotional Intelligence, remember, Star Seeker, that every journey starts with a single step. The path to Galactic Excellence isn't about leaping over cosmic gaps in a single bound but about consistent, forward motion, one planet, one star, one galaxy at a time. Let's dig deeper into these four Pillars, exploring ways to strengthen each one as we set the trajectory for your journey towards your North Star System.

《 》

Self-Awareness: Your Personal Observatory

Our exploration of the Four Pillars of Emotional Intelligence now brings us to the heart of the matter – your Personal Observatory, the realm of self-awareness. Just as an observatory's telescope points to the heavens to understand celestial bodies, your Personal Observatory helps you navigate the internal constellations of your emotions.

The path to your North Star System, to Galactic Excellence, must begin with understanding yourself - recognizing your emotions, understanding your strengths and vulnerabilities, and clarifying your needs and desires. This is the domain of self-awareness.

This is not always an easy voyage. Some of the constellations of our being can seem obscure, nebulous, or even threatening, akin to encountering a supermassive black hole. Yet, it is in these very challenges that the profoundest opportunities for growth and understanding lie.

The art of self-awareness involves tuning into your feelings at any given moment. It's about illuminating the dark matter of your being, making the invisible visible. It's about understanding that emotions, much like cosmic phenomena, are not inherently positive or negative. They simply are. They are clues to your deepest needs.

Through this enhanced understanding, you can start recognizing how your emotions drive your actions and influence the people around you. It's about discerning patterns, recognizing recurring meteor showers of particular emotions. Perhaps you feel a surge of frustration when a goal is obstructed or a sense of joy when you've assisted a fellow Star Seeker on their journey.

As you deepen your understanding of these patterns, you will also see how your emotions influence your decisions. A pattern of decision making guided by impulsive emotions may not always lead you towards your North Star System. Through the practice of self-awareness, you will be better equipped to take charge of these decisions.

Consider this section a star chart to your internal galaxy. It's about more than just recognizing emotions as they happen. It's about understanding their origins, their impact, and the trails they leave behind. It's about understanding yourself on a galactic level.

Remember, the path to self-awareness is not a sprint; it's a marathon—an interstellar marathon. As you explore your Personal Observatory, be patient with yourself. Be a compassionate observer of your inner world and recognize that every moment of awareness is a step forward in your journey to your North Star System.

⟪ ⟫

Self-Management: Mastering   Your Spacecraft Controls

In the vast cosmos of our emotions, self-awareness is our personal observatory. But being aware of our emotional cosmos is not the endpoint. It's merely the beginning. Once we understand the constellation of emotions within us, the next step is to effectively navigate through them. This is where self-management, or mastering your spacecraft controls, comes in.

Much like a seasoned astronaut handling the controls of their spacecraft, you too need to master the controls of your emotional universe. This isn't about suppressing or ignoring emotions but rather understanding them and managing their influence over your actions.

The goal isn't to escape the pull of your emotions, but rather to harness their energy productively. It's about achieving a state of emotional equilibrium where you can acknowledge your feelings without letting them dictate your behavior. This equilibrium allows us to handle stress, control impulses, and motivate ourselves—all essential skills on our journey towards the North Star System.

Consider an astronaut encountering a sudden asteroid storm. If they panic and act impulsively, they could endanger their spacecraft and their mission. But if they remain calm, acknowledging the threat but not allowing fear to override their training, they can navigate through the storm safely. This is the essence of self-management—having the capacity to manage our reactions in the face of emotional storms.

Practical strategies to master your spacecraft controls could include mindfulness techniques, such as breathing exercises or meditation. You could also use cognitive strategies like reframing negative thoughts or forecasting the consequences of impulsive actions. It could be as simple as taking a pause when you feel a strong emotion coming on, allowing yourself the space to choose your response.

Remember, emotions are not your enemy. They are powerful sources of information and energy. The key is to learn how to harness this energy rather than be overwhelmed by it. This section aims to equip you with practical tools to become a skilled astronaut of your emotional universe, using self-management to steer your way towards your North Star System.

We each have the capability to become masters of our own spacecraft, navigators of our emotional cosmos. Your journey to Galactic Excellence is not just about reaching your destination; it's also about growing and learning how to effectively navigate the cosmos within you. So, strap in and prepare to master your spacecraft controls. The journey to your North Star System awaits.

《 》

Social Awareness: Scanning the Intergalactic Environment

Our journey through the cosmos of emotional intelligence continues as we venture beyond our personal spacecraft and explore the wider intergalactic environment. You are not traveling alone in this vast universe; there are other Star Seekers, other explorers, each on their unique journey. This is where social awareness, or scanning the intergalactic environment, comes into play.

Imagine yourself at the helm of your spaceship, soaring through the infinite cosmos towards your North Star System. You are not just navigating through stars and planets, but also encountering other spacecraft and civilizations along the way. In these moments, understanding the emotions and needs of others becomes critical for ensuring a smooth journey.

Social awareness is about expanding the scope of your observatory to include not just your emotions but those of others as well. It's about picking up on emotional cues, understanding social dynamics, and recognizing the needs and concerns of other Star Seekers. It's the ability to walk a mile in another's spacesuit, understanding their perspective, and empathizing with their feelings.

Developing social awareness can feel like learning a new language – the language of emotions. And much like learning any language, it takes practice. It involves being present, actively listening, and observing body language. It means reading between the lines, understanding unspoken messages, and detecting subtleties in emotional cues. By tuning into these signals, you gain a better understanding of the emotional landscapes of others.

Why is this important? In our metaphorical cosmos, it's about co-existing harmoniously with other entities, respecting their space and their journey. In real life, it's about building meaningful relationships, fostering teamwork, and creating a positive social environment.

Whether it's at home, at work, or in the wider world, your ability to understand and respect the feelings of others is key to your journey towards Galactic Excellence.

By scanning the intergalactic environment and becoming attuned to the emotions of others, you can engage more effectively with the universe around you. Social awareness equips you to navigate complex social terrains and promotes interstellar harmony, allowing you to traverse the cosmos with grace and understanding. Embrace this skill, Star Seeker, for it is a crucial tool in your quest for your North Star System.

《 》

Relationship Management: Forming Cosmic Alliances

As we've navigated through the realms of self-awareness, self-management, and social awareness, you've undoubtedly grasped that our journey through this emotional cosmos is not a solitary one. We are part of a grand, interconnected universe of Star Seekers, each charting their own path towards their North Star System. Now, we move into the domain of relationship management - the ability to form and navigate cosmic alliances.

In the context of our cosmic voyage, relationship management is about fostering strong and beneficial alliances with other entities we meet along our journey. Just as spacecrafts form fleets to explore the cosmos together, we too need strong alliances in our own quests. But these alliances are not only about journeying together; they're about growing together, learning from one another, and supporting each other in times of stellar storms and asteroid impacts.

Emotional intelligence is the thruster that propels these alliances, and relationship management is the navigation system that guides them. It's about using our understanding of our own emotions and those of others to manage interactions successfully. This means clear communication, handling conflicts in a positive way, inspiring and influencing others, and working well in a team. It's about knowing when to lead, when to follow, and when to journey side-by-side.

The true skill of relationship management lies in the ability to harmonize our emotions with those of others. It's about creating an emotional resonance that benefits all parties involved. This doesn't mean suppressing your feelings for the sake of peace or disregarding the feelings of others for personal gain. Instead, it's about understanding, respecting, and balancing diverse emotional needs and responses.

Mastering relationship management and forming cosmic alliances requires practice and patience. There will be misunderstandings, there will be conflicts. But these challenges are not dead ends, they're learning opportunities, chances to learn more about ourselves and others. Remember, Star Seeker, even stars are born from chaos and collision.

So, Star Seeker, as you voyage through your emotional universe towards your True North Star, remember to invest in your cosmic alliances. These alliances will not only enrich your journey but also enhance your personal growth. Relationship management is a key aspect of emotional intelligence, and a powerful tool in your quest for Galactic Excellence. Cultivate it, nurture it, and you'll be one step closer to your cosmic destination.

《 》

Harnessing Dark Energy: The Power of Emotional Intelligence in Your Cosmic Journey

In the previous sections, we've unraveled the complexities of the four pillars of emotional intelligence. Now, it's time to harness the immense force of this dark energy, integrate it into our spacecraft's system, and let it propel us on our cosmic journey towards the North Star System.

Think of emotional intelligence as your cosmic fuel. Like the unseen dark energy that constitutes most of the universe, emotional intelligence often goes unrecognized. Yet, it's an extraordinary force, powering our journey, shaping our interstellar trajectory, and paving our path to Galactic Excellence.

The first step to harness this power is to realize that emotional intelligence isn't a fixed trait. It's a skill, a learned capability that grows and refines as we journey through the galaxy. It's never too late or too early to enhance your emotional intelligence. Your cosmic journey is unique, and so is your emotional development. Be patient, Star Seeker. Growth, like cosmic evolution, takes time.

Enhancing your emotional intelligence begins with observation and self-reflection. Dive into the depths of your personal observatory. Notice your emotions as they surface, acknowledge their presence, and try to understand what triggers them. This practice, though seemingly simple, is a powerful fuel for self-awareness.

As you grow more attuned to your emotions, start practicing self-management. When faced with an asteroid field of stress or an unexpected warp of anger, take a moment. Breathe. Channel the calm of the cosmic void. Rather than reacting impulsively, choose your response. You are the captain of your spaceship, the master of your journey.

Next, extend your sensors to the emotional signals of others. Practice empathy, trying to understand other Star Seekers from their perspective. Listen to their words, but also observe their non-verbal cues. Just as you'd study the behavior of an unknown cosmic entity, strive to comprehend the feelings of others.

Finally, use your understanding of emotions to build stronger cosmic alliances. Communicate openly, resolve conflicts constructively, and foster an environment of mutual respect and emotional resonance.

Harnessing the power of emotional intelligence isn't about suppressing your feelings or becoming emotionally 'neutral.' It's about understanding, managing, and utilizing your emotions constructively. It's about transforming the unseen dark energy of emotional intelligence into a guiding light for your cosmic journey.

Embrace the power of this dark energy, Star Seeker. Let it fuel your journey, guide your interactions, and propel you towards your True North Star. In this vast, interconnected cosmos, your emotional intelligence is an invaluable force, driving you closer to Galactic Excellence with every cosmic rotation.

$$\langle\!\langle\ \rangle\!\rangle$$

Illuminating the Dark Energy

As our cosmic voyage through the dark energy of emotional intelligence reaches its waypoint, it's time to pause and gaze at the galaxy around us. We've ventured deep into the unexplored realms of self-awareness, self-management, social awareness, and relationship management. We've unraveled the dark energy within us, learning to perceive its pulse, understand its currents, and guide its immense force towards our North Star System.

Remember, Star Seeker, as you journey through this vast cosmic tapestry, you are not just an observer. You are an active participant, shaping and being shaped by the interstellar journey. The dark energy of emotional intelligence is not an external force acting upon you. It's a part of you, an intrinsic component of your cosmic essence, echoing from the core of your Star Seeker spirit.

The path to Galactic Excellence is not a linear trajectory, but a dynamic orbit. It's a journey of continuous learning, growth, and transformation. And in this transformative process, your emotional intelligence is your navigator. It helps you understand your emotional gravity, master your celestial course, and maintain a harmonious resonance with fellow voyagers.

Embrace this dark energy within you, Star Seeker. Illuminate it with the light of understanding, acceptance, and compassion. Harness its power to propel your spacecraft, to navigate your interstellar interactions, and to fuel your pursuit of the North Star System.

And as you continue your cosmic journey, remember that each challenge you encounter, each asteroid field you navigate, and each alien civilization you connect with, will only enhance your emotional intelligence. Each experience is an opportunity to grow, to learn, and to harness the immense potential of your inner dark energy.

So, fear not the shadow of the dark energy. Instead, illuminate it. Embrace it. Harness it. And let this hidden force guide you on your quest for Galactic Excellence. Because the true Star Seeker understands that the unseen can be the most powerful force in their cosmic journey. And in the radiant heart of the unseen dark energy lies the path to your True North Star.

Chapter 4: The Event Horizon - Staring Down Failure's Black Hole

Grappling with the Gravity of Failure

Every Star Seeker, regardless of their velocity or direction, encounters the same ominous object in their cosmic voyage - the black hole of failure. There is a natural trepidation that binds us at the edge of this seemingly endless abyss. As ominous as it seems, we must face the inescapable truth: failure, much like the black hole, is a fundamental part of our universe.

Picture a black hole, a collapsed star. It possesses a gravitational force so strong that nothing, not even light, can escape its pull once it crosses the event horizon. Failure, in our journey, often feels akin to this overwhelming force, tugging at us relentlessly, attempting to swallow our dreams and aspirations. But what if we viewed failure not as an end, but a beginning? What if, like intrepid space explorers, we dared to stare into the inky void of failure and see it not as an insurmountable obstacle, but as a challenge to be conquered?

In our quest for Galactic Excellence, we must learn to confront the gravity of failure. Not to be consumed by it, but to understand it, learn from it, and ultimately, leverage it as a propellant on our cosmic journey. This chapter, fellow Star Seeker, aims to guide you on this daunting yet empowering part of your voyage as you learn to grapple with the gravity of failure and harness its hidden power.

《 》

The Fear of Falling: Understanding the Impact of Failure

Fear, as an emotion, is programmed into the very fabric of our being. It is a survival mechanism designed to protect us from danger. It alerts us to the presence of threats and compels us to take action. Yet, like a navigation system that has lost its calibration, fear can sometimes misdirect us, leading us to perceive threats where none exist. And this is where we encounter our first celestial quandary, the fear of failure or, as Star Seekers may refer to it, the Fear of Falling.

As we stare into the abyss of the black hole, it's not the descent itself that frightens us. It is the imagined aftermath: the failure. We fear the disappointment, the potential ridicule, the potential loss of respect, and most of all, we fear the perceived finality of failure. Our society, which often praises success and shuns failure, compounds this fear. We are led to believe that failure defines us, that it's an indelible stain on our cosmic journey that can never be washed away.

However, this belief couldn't be farther from the truth. Failure is not a dead end or a testament to our incompetence. Rather, it's a detour, a part of the learning process, a stepping-stone on the path to excellence. The impact of failure on our journey is largely determined by our perception of it. We can choose to let it drag us down, spiraling into the black hole of self-doubt and despair or we can use it as a launching pad, a source of invaluable insights and lessons to propel us towards our True North Star. The key lies in understanding our fear of failure, acknowledging its presence, and then consciously choosing to not let it steer our ship.

In the next section, we will explore practical strategies to help you face your fear of falling, embrace the lessons failure has to offer, and redefine its impact on your journey towards Galactic Excellence.

《 》

Cosmic Collisions: Learning from Setbacks

Let's continue our space journey with an intriguing observation. In the vast expanse of our cosmos, celestial bodies don't just float around in harmonious stillness. There are collisions, fiery and fierce, resulting in destruction, transformation, and paradoxically, creation. Similarly, our journey towards Galactic Excellence is not devoid of setbacks. We too, experience our share of cosmic collisions - our failures and mistakes.

However, these collisions, as tumultuous as they may be, are not merely destructive. Each collision, each setback, brings with it an opportunity for learning, transformation, and growth. Each failure, each misstep, contains valuable data, waiting to be discovered, analyzed, and applied in our cosmic journey.

If we think of our failures as intergalactic crash sites, then our task becomes one of a space archaeologist. We must sift through the debris not with despair but with curiosity, searching for clues, understanding what went wrong, and how we can prevent similar collisions in the future. Was it a miscalculation? A lapse in judgement? An unforeseen obstacle? Or perhaps a fault in our spaceship? Each answer, each newfound wisdom, strengthens our journey, equipping us better for the voyage ahead.

But, Star Seeker, **remember this**: the process of learning from setbacks requires humility and courage. Humility to admit that we can falter, and courage to face our shortcomings. It is only when we embrace our fallibility can we truly harness the wisdom that our failures have to offer.

Let's delve deeper into this concept in our next section, where we'll explore specific strategies to navigate setbacks and transform them into stepping stones towards your North Star.

⟨ ⟩

Resisting the Pull: Building Resilience

Ever marveled at how a comet, despite being drawn by the irresistible pull of a black hole, often resists succumbing entirely, using the gravitational energy to slingshot itself into a new trajectory? Resilience, Star Seeker, is your slingshot. It's the innate power that allows you to resist the crippling pull of failure's black hole, bounce back from setbacks, and even use them to propel you towards your North Star.

Understandably, the pull of failure can be powerful, daunting, and demoralizing. It tugs at your self-confidence, rattles your beliefs, and questions your competence. Yet, resilience is that indomitable force within you, that defies this gravitational pull, that says, "I shall not surrender. I shall rise, yet again."

Building resilience isn't about denying the existence of failure or cloaking it in a false sense of positivity. It's about accepting the setback, feeling the sting, yet refusing to let it define your journey. It's about holding onto hope when the horizon seems bleak, about learning from mistakes when confusion ensues, and about persevering when the path appears arduous.

So, how does one build resilience? Firstly, reframe your narrative. View setbacks as detours not dead ends. See failures as teachers not tormentors. Secondly, cultivate a growth mindset. Believe in your ability to learn, grow, and improve. See challenges as opportunities to expand your skills and understanding. Lastly, practice self-compassion. Be gentle with yourself when you falter. After all, even the most seasoned Star Seekers experience a stumble or two.

As we progress in this chapter, we will explore more practical strategies to enhance your resilience and navigate the uncertain terrain of setbacks. For now, remember that you, Star Seeker, are far stronger than you believe, far more capable than you know, and far more resilient than you imagine. Let us proceed on this journey with that empowering thought.

《 》

The Slingshot Maneuver: Using Failure to Propel Success

Astrophysics presents us with an amazing phenomenon known as the gravitational slingshot, also known as a gravity assist. Spacecraft use this technique to pick up speed by moving around a planet, utilizing its gravitational pull as a catapult. It's a spectacular dance of celestial bodies that demonstrates an incredibly inspiring principle: with the right maneuvers, forces that initially seem to pull us down can be harnessed to propel us forward.

Imagine your setbacks, your failures, as these celestial bodies. They're massive, powerful, and exert a significant pull on your journey. They may seem to hinder your progress, dragging you into their event horizons. But what if you could use this pull to your advantage? This is the essence of the slingshot maneuver.

The slingshot maneuver in your quest for Galactic Excellence involves three critical steps: embrace, evaluate, and evolve.

Firstly, **embrace** your failure. This doesn't mean you should desire or enjoy failing, but rather acknowledge when it occurs. Resist the urge to escape its gravity prematurely or deny its existence. Remember, there's no slingshot without the gravitational pull.

Next, **evaluate** your experience. Ask yourself: What did this setback teach me? What could I have done differently? These questions aren't meant to fuel self-doubt, but to generate insight. This evaluation allows you to transform the gravitational force of failure into kinetic energy for your journey.

Finally, **evolve**. Use the lessons you've learned to inform your future actions. This is the moment of release, where you use the accumulated energy to propel you forward, towards your True North Star.

Remember, Star Seeker, the aim isn't to avoid the gravity of failure altogether, for that's an inescapable part of any cosmic journey. Instead, our goal is to master the slingshot maneuver - to embrace, evaluate, and evolve from our failures, using their force not as a deterrent, but as a catapult towards our desired destination. Onward and upward, we continue our celestial journey, not despite our setbacks, but empowered by them.

$$\langle\!\langle\ \rangle\!\rangle$$

F ailures, Not Final: Changing Our Perception of Failure

Aboard this cosmic voyage, we have charted the course of failure, from the fear of falling to resilience and the dynamic slingshot maneuver. However, our navigation through failure's black hole would be incomplete without addressing one of the most critical aspects – the transformation of our perceptions about failure.

Our societies, quite unfortunately, often program us to see failure as a devastating end, as a final destination where dreams come to perish. Yet, in the grand expanse of the universe, even stars in their deaths give birth to new elements, nebulas, and sometimes, black holes that become the cradles of galaxies. If the cosmos itself can transform such cataclysmic events into beginnings of new creations, can we not also adapt our perceptions of personal failures?

Let's reorient our thinking, Star Seekers. Let us shift our gaze from the crushing weight of the black hole to the explosive brilliance of the quasar. Yes, failures may come with pain, disappointment, and regret. But they're also saturated with lessons, resilience, and invaluable growth. In our quest for Galactic Excellence, it's imperative that we change our vision of failure from a terminal point to a formative event, from an 'end' to a 'beginning.'

Each failure you encounter on your journey is not a sign of finality but an opportunity for transformation. They're akin to the birth pangs of a new star being born out of a collapsing nebula. Painful, yes, but also incredibly beautiful and necessary for the emergence of something brighter, stronger, and more refined.

Consider each setback, each stumble, not as a blockade but as a stepping-stone on your interstellar path. Much like a star, let every collapse forge you, not finish you. Let every failure be the crucible in which your Galactic Excellence is refined and reshaped.

Remember, Star Seeker, failure is only 'final' if you allow it to be. The universe is not a place of finality but of continuous creation, evolution, and transformation. In this limitless expanse, even black holes are not the end – they are the mysterious gateways to other cosmic possibilities. So too, let each of your failures be a gateway, not a final destination, on your magnificent journey towards your North Star. Let each setback shape you, grow you, and ultimately, guide you on your path to Galactic Excellence. The universe is ever-changing, and so too is the journey of a true Star Seeker.

《 》

Turning the Event Horizon into a Launchpad

As we stand at the precipice of this chapter, on the rim of the fearsome event horizon, we look back at our voyage through failure's black hole. It's been a journey punctuated by turbulence and setbacks, challenges, and learning. However, the crucial essence of our exploration resides not in the pull of the black hole, but in our courageous endeavor to resist it, learn from it, and ultimately, use its force to propel us further into our cosmic quest.

Indeed, the power of a Star Seeker lies not in avoiding black holes but in mastering their art – the art of turning an event horizon into a launchpad.

Much like a spaceship using the intense gravity of a planet to catapult itself deeper into space, we too can utilize the formidable power of our failures to slingshot ourselves towards success. We can turn the point of no return into a point of rebirth, a place where old strategies, ideas, and approaches collapse under the weight of their own shortcomings to give birth to new, refined, and stronger ones.

Yes, the event horizon is intimidating. But remember, Star Seeker, it is not the sight of the horizon that matters; it's the perspective with which you view it. Will you see it as a final barrier, an insurmountable obstacle, or will you see it as an opportunity, a launchpad?

Let the event horizon be your turning point. Embrace the pull, understand its power, and then, with all your might, turn that power on its head. Use it to fuel your voyage towards Galactic Excellence. Let every failure be your motivator, every setback your teacher, and every fear your navigational guide.

As we close this chapter, look at the cosmic mirror and see yourself not as a victim of a black hole, but as a resilient, resourceful Star Seeker – one who not only dares to stare down the event horizon but also has the audacity to use it as a launchpad.

Remember, the cosmos favors the brave, the resilient, the learners. By embracing your failures, by staring down the black hole, and by using its gravity as your propellant, you are not only setting your course for the North Star but also becoming a beacon of inspiration for all the Star Seekers charting their course through this infinite, beautiful cosmos. Failure, Star Seeker, is not the end. It is, indeed, the beginning. And so, as we look back one last time at the event horizon, we realize that we've already begun our journey into a brighter, more brilliant tomorrow. Onwards, to Galactic Excellence

Chapter 5: Harnessing the Power of a Quasar - Willpower, Your Starship's Fuel

The Quasar Within

As our cosmic journey continues to unfurl across the galaxies, the celestial landscape unveils yet another source of extraordinary power and light. Quasars are the brightest objects in the universe with a luminosity a thousand times greater than our Milky Way galaxy. These interstellar giants, though remote and distant, carry a profound message for every Star Seeker. For within each of us lies an innate force as compelling and potent as a quasar. This is your willpower.

Just as a quasar emanates its light from the core, drawing its energy from the supermassive black hole it surrounds, willpower too radiates from deep within us, originating from the core of our being. It is a personal power source, a well of strength that illuminates our path and pushes us forward, even in the darkest corners of space or the most challenging phases of our journey.

Our internal quasar—our willpower—is a beacon of resilience and determination. It fuels our commitment to stay on course, to remain resolute in our mission, to transcend the pull of setbacks, to navigate the unpredictable and the unknown. It enables us to take leaps of faith into the uncharted territories of our personal cosmos, reminding us that we are more than just stardust, we are starlight too. We are Star Seekers.

As we delve deeper into the mysteries of willpower, you will discover how this extraordinary energy source can be harnessed, nurtured, and directed towards your quest for Galactic Excellence. Like the quasar that illuminates the cosmos, your willpower has the potential to outshine any obstacle that dares to eclipse your North Star. So, buckle up, Star Seeker, it's time to light up your inner quasar and unleash the strength of your willpower. Let us set a course for this illuminating journey of self-discovery.

《 》

Galactic Gale: The Winds of Willpower

Just as the galactic winds shape nebulae and carve pathways through interstellar dust, your willpower shapes the trajectory of your quest, pushing against the obstacles and carving your path towards Galactic Excellence. It is an unseen, yet palpable force, a continuous gust of determination that propels your spacecraft forward, even against the harshest cosmic storms.

The strength of the galactic winds does not lie merely in their intensity, but also in their persistence. They blow ceaselessly, sculpting and influencing the celestial landscapes over the eons. Likewise, the strength of willpower is not merely about the intensity of your determination in a single moment, but also about the persistent application of that determination over time. It is about your ability to stay the course, your unwavering commitment to reach your North Star, your continuous striving for Galactic Excellence, no matter how long the journey or how formidable the challenges.

Just as the galactic winds embrace and journey through the cosmic chaos, creating awe-inspiring formations of stellar beauty, you too, as a Star Seeker, should harness the winds of your willpower to embrace your challenges. Turn the chaos of your trials into stepping stones, shaping your journey towards a future that resonates with your true self, an inspiring testament to your courage, resilience, and will.

In this section, we will explore how to generate and harness this 'Galactic Gale,' this willpower within you. You will learn how to maintain its persistence and how to navigate it towards your desired direction. We will delve into strategies that can keep your willpower strong and constant, helping you sail smoothly even when cosmic storms try to veer you off your path.

So, Star Seeker, ready your sails. Let the Galactic Gale of your willpower guide you, reshape your landscape, and propel you towards your North Star. Unleash the wind of determination, and let it fill your journey with the promise of discovery and Galactic Excellence. The cosmos is vast, but remember, so is the strength of your will. Let's set forth and harness the Power of your Quasar.

《 》

The Cosmic Fuel: Understanding the Role of Willpower

Willpower acts as the cosmic fuel for your starship on this grand voyage to Galactic Excellence. It is the driving force behind your determination and resilience, the energy source that allows you to travel vast cosmic distances, from the familiar constellations of your comfort zone to the uncharted galaxies of growth and potential.

Consider this: Every spacecraft requires a source of propulsion to overcome the gravitational forces that tether it to the ground. In the case of our interstellar journey, the ground is our present state – our current skills, beliefs, and habits. The gravitational force we face is the resistance to change, the allure of comfort, the fear of the unknown. And the propulsion that enables us to overcome this resistance, that propels us out of our comfort zone and into the stellar expanse of growth, is our willpower.

Just as the spacecraft uses its fuel to generate the thrust needed for lift-off, you use your willpower to generate the thrust for your 'liftoff' – to start your journey, to take the first steps towards your North Star. And just as the spacecraft continues to burn fuel to sustain its flight and navigate the cosmos, you continue to harness your willpower to sustain your progress and navigate your path to Galactic Excellence.

But remember, Star Seeker, willpower is more than just a 'kick-starter' for your journey. It's the powerhouse that fuels your resilience, enabling you to weather the cosmic storms and meteor showers of challenges and setbacks that are an inherent part of any journey. It is the strength that enables you to hold course when you encounter the black holes of failure and doubt, to remain steadfast in your quest, and to continue moving towards your North Star.

Understanding the function of willpower in your journey is vital. It's about recognizing the potential energy within you, waiting to be tapped into. It's about understanding the power you hold to shape your own destiny, to chart your course through the celestial map of life.

⟨ ⟩

The Depleting Reservoir: Managing Your Willpower

A quasar, one of the most powerful entities in the universe, emits unfathomable energy. It is a beacon of raw power, illuminating the cosmos with its dazzling light. However, even a quasar, with its tremendous output, follows the universal rule of energy conservation. Its energy is not infinite, and one day, it will exhaust its fuel and fade away.

In a similar vein, our willpower is like the energy of a quasar, a reservoir of driving force. But just like a quasar, our willpower is not an inexhaustible resource. It can be depleted. Each decision we make, each resistance we overcome, each step we take on our journey to Galactic Excellence consumes a portion of our willpower.

Imagine your willpower as the fuel tank of your starship. Every cosmic storm weathered, every asteroid field navigated, every black hole evaded drains your tank a little more. And like any fuel tank, it needs to be refilled regularly to ensure a smooth and continued journey.

But worry not, fellow Star Seeker, this does not signal the end of our journey. Not by a long shot. Our cosmic journey is not a sprint; it's a marathon—a prolonged voyage through the cosmos. To successfully navigate this journey, we must learn to manage our willpower effectively, replenishing it as needed, and conserving it for when we need it the most.

In this section, we will explore some strategies for effectively managing your willpower. We will learn how to refill your reservoir, to ensure you never find yourself stranded in the cosmic void. We will discover how to pace yourself, conserving your willpower for the longest stretches of your journey. And we will understand how to maximize your fuel efficiency, using less willpower to achieve more.

《 》

Stellar Drive: How Willpower Moves You Forward

Our willpower, our internal quasar, serves a purpose. It's the celestial fuel that powers our stellar drive, the intrinsic motivation that pushes us forward in our cosmic journey. Willpower and motivation, intertwined like binary stars, are the twin engines that drive our starship towards Galactic Excellence.

Yet, these two forces, while symbiotic, are distinct. Willpower is the resource we tap into, the fuel for our starship, while motivation is the destination we set for ourselves, the North Star System that we navigate towards. But how do these twin engines of willpower and motivation interact? And how do they propel us forward in our cosmic journey?

When our starship encounters a cosmic storm, it is the motivation that directs us to brace for it, to navigate through it. It is the desire to reach our North Star System, the yearning for Galactic Excellence, that steers us. Yet, it is our willpower that powers our thrusters, enabling us to weather the storm and press on.

When we come across an asteroid field, it is the motivation that decides we must cross it, that behind this obstacle lies our path towards Galactic Excellence. And it is our willpower that fuels our deflector shields, letting us traverse through the field unscathed.

In the face of a daunting black hole, it is the motivation that makes us refuse to be pulled in, to not give up on our quest for Galactic Excellence. And it is our willpower that accelerates our escape, enabling us to resist the pull and slingshot past the black hole.

In each scenario, motivation provides the direction, and willpower provides the drive. They are a cosmic duo, powering our starship and charting our course towards Galactic Excellence. This inseparable relationship between willpower and motivation is what propels us forward, pushes us to venture into the unexplored, and drives us to overcome the insurmountable.

So, Star Seeker, let your willpower fuel your starship. Set your sights on your North Star System and let your motivation guide you. As we continue our cosmic journey, **remember this**: Your willpower and motivation, together, are your Stellar Drive, the force that moves you forward towards Galactic Excellence.

《 》

Supernova Strength: Strengthening Your Willpower

Just as a supernova represents the breathtaking crescendo of a star's life, its power echoing through the cosmos, strengthening your willpower can lead to a similar explosion of potential within your own life. This newfound supernova strength, when harnessed, can empower your journey toward Galactic Excellence like no other force can.

The universe has a spectacular way of demonstrating that extraordinary power often emerges from seemingly ordinary celestial bodies, and similarly, Star Seekers, your willpower—a force as ordinary as it is potent—has the potential to become your internal supernova. But how can you ignite this force? How can you harness your willpower to serve your journey effectively?

Begin with small steps. A supernova doesn't occur overnight; it's the result of a star's gradual, yet relentless, accumulation of energy. Similarly, strengthening your willpower isn't about making sweeping, drastic changes all at once. Instead, it's about the cumulative effect of small, manageable decisions and actions taken consistently over time.

For instance, consider setting micro-goals. These are small, achievable objectives that build toward your larger goal of Galactic Excellence. Meeting these micro-goals, step by step, day by day, will not only give you a sense of accomplishment but also train your willpower, gradually fortifying it.

Next, practice mindfulness. The most powerful telescope at a Star Seeker's disposal is their mind. It is through conscious awareness and intentional mindfulness that you can perceive the state of your willpower, understand its fluctuations, and predict its ebbs and flows. By becoming more aware of how your willpower works, you can manage it more effectively and prevent it from being depleted.

Lastly, remember the importance of rest. Just as a star needs time to gather energy before its explosive transformation into a supernova, your willpower too needs time to recharge. This could mean taking regular breaks during challenging tasks, getting plenty of sleep, or engaging in activities that rejuvenate you.

By following these steps, you're not only strengthening your willpower—you're also preparing for the moment when your internal quasar turns into a supernova, propelling you with an immense burst of energy toward your North Star System. So, Star Seekers, summon your Supernova Strength. Through consistency, mindfulness, and rest, let your willpower explode into a force as compelling and as influential as a supernova.

《 》

The Gravity Well: When Willpower Is Not Enough

Even the most powerful of quasars, or the most focused beams of stellar willpower, can falter when confronted by the immense force of a gravity well. In this universe, there exist forces so powerful and all-consuming that even willpower, our Starship's most robust fuel, may not be enough. Star Seekers, in your journey, you too may encounter such gravity wells, moments where your willpower alone may not suffice.

However, these gravitational pulls are not to be feared but understood. They represent those times in life when resistance is high, when goals seem unreachable, and when every step feels like a monumental task. In these moments, relying solely on willpower can feel akin to a spacecraft attempting to escape a black hole using only its engines, an exhausting and, often, futile endeavor.

Yet, there is hope. There are ways to navigate these gravity wells that do not solely depend on your willpower. These tools—habit formation and environmental design—are like the ingenious technologies on your starship that help you maintain course even in the face of the most formidable gravitational force.

Habit formation is akin to programming your starship's autopilot. When a behavior becomes a habit, it no longer requires the active engagement of your willpower. This process liberates your willpower reserves, enabling them to be used where they are needed the most. Therefore, cultivating beneficial habits can be a powerful strategy in your quest for Galactic Excellence.

Consider, for example, your goal to study the cosmic languages. Instead of relying on sheer willpower every day, you can develop a habit. Set a specific time each day dedicated to this task, make it a routine, and soon your starship will automatically navigate towards this activity, minimizing the need for willpower.

Environmental design, on the other hand, refers to altering the space around you to reduce the gravitational pull of distractions and obstacles. It involves arranging your physical and mental environment in a way that naturally guides your actions towards your goals. This could mean decluttering your study area or setting up reminders of your goals in visible places.

Think of your environment as the gravitational fields that surround your starship. By designing it to support your journey instead of hinder it, you create a path of least resistance, helping you conserve your willpower.

Yes, there will be gravity wells on your journey to Galactic Excellence. Yes, there will be moments when even your willpower may falter. However, remember, Star Seeker, that you are equipped with more than just willpower. You have at your disposal the power of habit and the ability to design your environment. So, engage these tools, navigate the gravity wells, and continue your journey through the cosmos, knowing that you are ever closer to your North Star System.

〈 〉

Willpower – Your Cosmic Propellant

In this journey, we have navigated through quasars and gravity wells, marveling at the incredible power of the universe and our own internal forces. As we draw this chapter to a close, let's reflect on the energy source propelling us forward: our willpower, our cosmic propellant.

Akin to the illuminating quasar, your willpower is a beacon of light that energizes your starship in the vast expanse of space. It fuels your voyage, motivates you to breach the unexplored, and propels you beyond the boundaries of your comfort galaxies. It is this unyielding force that is your most reliable companion in your quest for Galactic Excellence.

Throughout this chapter, we've explored how willpower functions as a resource, a powerful yet finite cosmic fuel. Just as a quasar radiates energy, your willpower drives your endeavors, but it can deplete and needs careful management and periodic recharging.

We delved into strategies for managing and replenishing this resource, uncovering ways to make our willpower glow with the ferocity of a supernova. By understanding how to harness this force, you've gained the knowledge to traverse challenging cosmic terrains and weather galactic storms.

But we also acknowledged the existence of gravity wells, those times when willpower alone might fall short. Here, we discovered the additional tools of habit formation and environmental design, giving you more comprehensive strategies to stay your course in your cosmic journey.

Star Seeker, remember, willpower is your cosmic propellant, your guiding starlight, your quasar within. Nurture it, replenish it, and respect its power. But also, remember that it is part of a broader toolkit for your journey. Combining willpower, habit formation, and environmental design will ensure that you are not only ready but eager to embark on each new leg of your journey towards Galactic Excellence.

As we venture further, continue to reflect on the lessons of this chapter. Nurture your internal quasar, feed it with positivity, and channel its energy towards your aspirations. Star Seeker, let's embark on this cosmic journey, for our starship is fueled, and our course set towards Galactic Excellence! Our voyage through this vast cosmos continues, and with willpower as our guide, there is no limit to the galaxies we can explore.

Chapter 6: Catching Stardust - Seizing Opportunities and Making Your Own Luck

Cosmic Stardust – The Opportunistic Particles

Imagine for a moment, your spaceship cutting a path through the silent, infinite expanse of the cosmos. Look closely at the infinitesimal particles of stardust that glimmer in the soft lights of your starship, dancing and swirling in a timeless cosmic ballet. This stardust represents the opportunities scattered across our paths, twinkling invitations, enticing us to reach out, capture, and incorporate them into our journey.

Just as the universe bursts with these particles of potential, our lives too are filled with glimmers of possibility, opportunities that can illuminate our course towards Galactic Excellence. Yet, the stardust of opportunity is elusive, dancing away on the solar winds if not swiftly captured. You, Star Seeker, need to be swift, your net of awareness cast wide to collect these precious particles. For within each speck of stardust lies the potential to propel your journey forward, to illuminate your path, and to power your progression towards your North Star.

As we venture further into this chapter, remember, each particle of stardust holds promise and possibility. It is our task to perceive, pursue, and encapsulate them within the confines of our spaceship, integrating them into the fuel that powers our galactic journey.

《 》

C elestial Recognition: Identifying Opportunities

The glow of a supernova or the ring of a pulsar can command our attention. Yet, amid the brilliant and the breathtaking, the seemingly insignificant stardust can be easily overlooked. This is the cosmic conundrum that the Star Seeker faces—how do we discern the invaluable particles of opportunity from the celestial vastness?

Much like the trained eyes of an astronomer recognizing patterns of stars and galaxies amid the cosmic clutter, your awareness and attention are the primary tools in identifying opportunities. By developing an acuity for the unusual, the promising, or the fortuitous, you learn to see the unseen, to detect the glimmering stardust amid the cosmic dust clouds.

It's a skill that demands curiosity and courage—curiosity to explore the unfamiliar paths, to probe the celestial shadows, and courage to step beyond the comfort zones, to dare to follow a different trajectory. As the universe teems with these particles of potential, it is essential to remain vigilant, patient, and discerning. Know that not every speck of stardust is meant for your journey; the key is to perceive those that align with your path and hold the potential to spur you forward.

Visualize yourself not just as an observer but as an active participant in the cosmic dance, attuned to the rhythm and the pace, understanding the ebb and flow of the galactic tide. Encourage yourself to ask questions, to seek answers, and to explore. Recognize the potential hidden in the challenges and the lessons concealed in failure. Be open to new ideas and perspectives, for they might be the stardust waiting to be captured.

⟨ ⟩

Galactic Grab: Seizing Opportunities

Having recognized the twinkling stardust of opportunity, the next phase in your celestial journey is to seize it, to reach out into the cosmic winds and close your fingers around the promising particles. However, bear in mind that capturing stardust is not an act of desperate grasping, but a careful and deliberate move, a dance choreographed by intent, will, and action.

Every opportune stardust particle you identify in your cosmic journey is surrounded by an ether of possibilities and probabilities, much like the swirling celestial winds around a particle of stardust. These are the conditions, circumstances, or even the occasional serendipity that can either propel the stardust within your reach or blow it into oblivion. Being in sync with these swirling winds is what allows a successful stardust capture.

The first step in this process is the readiness to act. Just as a seasoned astronomer is ready at all times to witness a rare celestial event, you need to be prepared to act when opportunities arise. This readiness comes from a place of self-confidence, from the belief that you have the potential and the capability to catch and hold onto the opportune stardust.

Next is the audacity to reach out, to make your move despite the risks and uncertainties. Remember, Star Seeker, risk and reward are often two sides of the same celestial body. The winds may be harsh, the stardust elusive, but it's your conviction and courage that will see you through.

Finally, it's the agility to adapt. The cosmic winds are ever-changing, opportunities morphing from one form to another. You must be willing to pivot, to change your course or strategy based on the dynamic cosmic conditions. Be flexible in your approach, innovative in your methods, and resilient in your pursuit.

The act of catching stardust, much like your journey towards Galactic Excellence, is not a linear process. It's a dance, a dynamic give-and-take with the universe. There will be misses, near-catches, and triumphant captures. Yet with each attempt, you hone your skills, increase your understanding of the cosmic rhythm, and move ever closer to your ultimate goal. So, Star Seekers, get ready to dance with the universe, reach out, and claim your stardust.

$$\langle\!\langle \ \rangle\!\rangle$$

Stardust Alchemy: Creating Opportunities

Once we've explored the art of capturing stardust, we now turn our gaze towards a more proactive approach, one that truly embodies the pioneering spirit of a Star Seeker—creating our own stardust, forging opportunities from the cosmic crucible itself.

Creating opportunities, Star Seeker, is akin to celestial alchemy. It's about transforming the ordinary elements of our existence into golden chances for growth and progress. It is this ability to create stardust that differentiates a passive traveler from an active Star Seeker on the cosmic journey.

This celestial alchemy doesn't happen by chance, nor does it depend on some mysterious cosmic lottery. Rather, it's rooted in the conscious choices we make, the endeavors we undertake, and the innovative ideas we bring into existence. Think of it as shaping your cosmic clay, molding it into opportunities, and then firing it in the kiln of effort and determination to create your unique stardust.

Consider the metaphor of a nebula, a vast cloud of gas and dust in outer space. Seemingly inert, it's these nebulas that serve as stellar nurseries, giving birth to new stars and their planetary systems. Similarly, what might seem like mere dust and gas in your life, your skills, experiences, and even challenges, can serve as the nebula for your new opportunities. By putting in energy and nurturing these elements, you can ignite the birth of new stars, opportunities that light up your journey towards Galactic Excellence.

To create such opportunities, it's crucial to adopt a mindset of growth and abundance. Embrace the cosmic uncertainty and have faith in your ability to navigate through it. Take risks, challenge the status quo, and be ready to step outside your comfort orbit. Remember, it's only when you venture into the unexplored cosmos that you discover new celestial bodies and phenomena.

Cultivate a sense of curiosity and continuous learning. Keep your sensors tuned for the ever-evolving cosmic knowledge and insights. The more you know, the better equipped you are to identify potential stardust in the rough.

Finally, network with fellow Star Seekers. Every celestial body in this cosmos, every Star Seeker, has a unique trajectory, a unique perspective. By connecting with them, you not only broaden your own cosmic understanding but also increase the chances of cross-pollination of ideas, giving birth to new stardust particles of opportunity.

As Star Seekers, let us not just passively navigate through the cosmos, hoping to stumble upon stardust. Let's engage in celestial alchemy, turning the raw cosmic matter into opportunities, and truly making our own luck.

《 》

Riding the Cosmic Winds: The Role of Preparedness

As we navigate this journey, weaving through celestial bodies and reaching for stardust, there's an invisible force at play, a silent ally that's often overlooked but deeply integral to our success. It's the underpinning factor in our ability to recognize, seize, and create opportunities: Preparedness.

Just as the winds of the cosmos, unseen yet powerful, direct the stardust to its destination, the winds of preparedness guide us towards opportunities. To ride these cosmic winds successfully, we need our spaceship—our self—to be in prime condition, fueled up and ready to make the leap when the time comes.

Recognizing opportunities is like spotting a faint star in the vast cosmic canopy. It requires an observant eye, a telescope fine-tuned to the specific wavelength of that star—your goals and ambitions. To be prepared is to keep this telescope ready, calibrated and focused, so that when the star—opportunity—appears, you can discern it amidst the cosmic noise.

Similarly, seizing opportunities can feel as challenging as capturing stardust on the fly. It's not enough to spot the stardust; we need the agility, the dexterity, and the precision to catch it. These traits are built over time, through consistent practice and proactive readiness. When an opportunity comes hurtling your way, if you're prepared, you can extend your cosmic net and catch that valuable stardust.

Finally, creating opportunities—our stardust alchemy—requires a comprehensive understanding of the cosmic elements and forces at play. It involves skill, creativity, and the courage to venture into the uncharted. Preparedness, in this context, means having the tools and knowledge at your disposal, refining your skills, and maintaining an innovative mindset that's always ready to challenge the cosmic norms.

Preparedness isn't about predicting every possible eventuality in our cosmic journey. The universe, with its infinite possibilities, makes that task near impossible. Rather, it's about developing a state of readiness, a flexible mindset that can adapt and respond to whatever the cosmos presents. It's about cultivating a broad skill set that can navigate through any celestial storm, and a spirit resilient enough to bounce back from the gravitational pull of setbacks.

So how do we cultivate this cosmic preparedness? Through continuous learning, curiosity, and practice. Keep your starship fueled with knowledge, skills, and experiences. Embrace a mindset of growth and adaptability, ready to take on new challenges and learn from them. Keep your navigation systems updated and adaptable, for the cosmos is an ever-changing entity. And most importantly, believe in your Star Seeker abilities. Your willpower, resilience, and the lessons you've learned from the event horizon of failure are all parts of your preparedness kit.

As we catch stardust and make our own luck, remember that riding the cosmic winds of preparedness is crucial. Opportunities may be scattered across the cosmos, but it's our readiness to spot, seize, and create them that truly fuels our journey towards Galactic Excellence.

$$\langle\!\langle\ \rangle\!\rangle$$

The Nebula Effect: From Stardust to Stars

We've embarked on an incredible quest, catching stardust and transforming it into a legacy of cosmic proportions. But you may wonder, how do these minute particles, these seized opportunities, coalesce into something as brilliant and significant as a star? Welcome to the marvel of the 'Nebula Effect.'

Nebulas are stellar nurseries, places where the seemingly innocuous stardust congregates under the force of gravity. Over time, these particles fuse together, birth heat and light, and eventually blossom into radiant stars. So, it is with the opportunities we seize; they may appear insignificant on their own, but when brought together, they create something remarkable.

Each opportunity we capture is a particle of stardust. On its own, it may seem tiny, barely noticeable in the grand scheme of our quest. But it holds within it the potential to contribute to a star—to a significant outcome or success. The key lies in aggregation and synergy.

Every seized opportunity, every speck of stardust, brings with it experiences, lessons, connections, and possibilities. As we accumulate these particles, they begin to interact, to learn from each other, to strengthen each other. Lessons from one opportunity inform decisions about the next. Connections from one encounter open doors to new experiences. Each success breeds confidence for the next challenge.

This process is not instantaneous. Just as a star doesn't form overnight, the aggregation and maturation of opportunities require patience and persistence. There will be times when the stardust seems to disperse, when the gravitational pull of doubt and failure attempt to disrupt the process. But remember, Star Seeker, it is in these moments that we must harness our willpower, draw on our resilience, and let the lessons we learned from the event horizon guide us.

Navigating the nebula of opportunity isn't a straightforward journey—it's an art. It's about finding the right balance between seizing the opportunities at hand and creating new ones, between maintaining focus on the present while keeping an eye on the future. It requires you to be agile, prepared, and resilient, constantly recalibrating your course based on the cosmic conditions.

Embrace the Nebula Effect. Gather your stardust. Nurture it, let it interact and grow, and watch in awe as it transforms into the bright, shining stars of your success. This is the essence of your journey—catching stardust, turning opportunities into outcomes, and lighting up your corner of the cosmos.

《 》

S tellar Luck: The Intersection of Preparedness and Opportunity

'Fortune favors the bold,' the ancients said, but as Star Seekers, we understand that fortune—or as we call it, 'stellar luck'—favors those who are prepared and perceptive. Stellar luck is the spectacular celestial display when a comet of opportunity intersects with the orbit of our preparedness.

Stellar luck is not merely the absence of misfortune; it's not about evading meteor showers or avoiding black holes. It's about actively positioning ourselves where opportunities are likely to emerge and being ready to seize them when they do. It's about aligning our cosmic trajectory with the path of stardust and having our nets ready to catch it.

You see, opportunities are much like celestial bodies in the cosmos. They have their orbits, their trajectories. They follow certain patterns and they tend to show up in certain places. If we position ourselves in these paths, if we align ourselves with these trajectories, we're far more likely to encounter these opportunities.

Preparedness is adding higher quality rocket fuel to our engines, accelerating us towards these paths, these celestial intersections. It's the time spent in the simulator, the hours spent studying the star maps, the effort put into understanding the cosmic conditions. It's the resilience developed from staring down the event horizon and the willpower harnessed from the power of a quasar.

And then, when an opportunity—a particle of stardust—does cross our path, we're ready. We know what it looks like, we know how to catch it, and we know how to make the most of it. That's when the magic happens. That's when stellar luck shines brightest.

Contrary to what the term may suggest, stellar luck is not left to chance. It's an active process, a journey of positioning and preparation. It's a testament to the truth that luck isn't just about being in the right place at the right time, but also about being the right person at that time.

Star Seeker, we don't wait for luck to come to us. We chart our course, we prepare for the journey, and we go out and meet it. We venture into the cosmic vastness, nets in hand, eyes on the stars, hearts full of hope. We catch the stardust, create our opportunities, and make our own stellar luck.

《 》

The Stardust Collection

In this grand celestial theatre, stardust - opportunities - are the golden threads that weave the cosmic tapestry of our journey. As we find ourselves looking back at the footprints we've left on the starlit canvas, it's the stardust we've gathered that gleams the brightest, leading us ever forward towards Galactic Excellence.

Throughout our journey, we've come to understand that opportunities, like stardust, are a shared resource of the cosmos. Yet it takes a certain fortitude, a keen eye, and a willing heart to truly perceive them. We've learned that spotting these twinkling particles amid the galactic expanse isn't a mere coincidence, but a skill to be honed, a sense to be sharpened. The cosmic radar that we've developed allows us to see, not just with our eyes, but with our intuition, our wisdom, our experience.

We've come to see that opportunity is not just about being at the right place at the right time. It is about making the right decisions, acting with resolve when a speck of stardust passes by, and courageously extending our hands to grasp it. It's about understanding that seizing opportunities involves making choices, taking risks, and sometimes, leaving the familiar path to venture into uncharted space.

Yet, we've discovered that not all stardust is found; some is created. We've cultivated the celestial craft of alchemizing challenges into opportunities, crafting our own stardust from the cosmic raw materials at our disposal. We've learned to forge particles of possibility from the meteors of adversity and comets of change, adding to our growing stardust collection.

The stardust we've caught and created along our journey does not just make our course more luminous, but it fundamentally shapes us. Each particle of opportunity seized and created molds us into better navigators of the cosmos, altering our trajectory towards ever brighter galaxies.

As we stand on the precipice of the next phase of our journey, let's take a moment to gaze at our stardust collection - a tangible testament to our journey, each particle a chapter of our cosmic story. We've gathered a great deal thus far, yet the cosmos is vast and stardust abounds. There are many particles yet to be caught, many opportunities yet to be seized, and many more yet to be created.

Chapter 7: Quantum Entanglement - The Unified Field of Teamwork and Leadership

Quantum Threads of Connectivity

Our universe is a place of profound interconnectedness, a network of inextricable threads. This complex network isn't limited to the celestial bodies that glide through the cosmos. On a quantum level, invisible bonds stitch together particles in an enigmatic dance. This phenomenon, known as quantum entanglement, creates a link so strong that the state of one particle instantaneously affects the other, no matter the distance between them. It's as if, across light-years of empty space, these tiny fragments of existence whisper to each other in a language only they understand.

In our quest for Galactic Excellence, we, the Star Seekers, are not unlike these quantumly entangled particles. Though we may seem like solitary voyagers, traversing our unique paths, we are, in truth, bound together in the intricate dance of success and growth. The threads of connectivity run deep, uniting us in shared goals, mutual respect, and collaborative efforts.

Much like quantum entanglement, our individual actions and decisions have far-reaching implications on the collective journey. Every choice we make, every triumph, every stumble, sends ripples through the fabric of our shared mission. We are united in our quest, each a crucial point of light in the constellation of progress.

Welcome to a new dimension of understanding. A dimension where we realize our shared pursuit does not entail a loss of individuality but a recognition of our collective power. It's the dimension of quantum entanglement, the unified field of teamwork and leadership, where we acknowledge that we are indeed stardust, but together, we form galaxies. So, let us embark on this journey together, exploring the vast cosmos of collaboration, leadership, and shared success.

《 》

Space-Time Synchronization: The Art of Communication

In the vast cosmos, space-time, the invisible fabric that cradles the universe, is the fundamental unit of existence. It governs the motion of galaxies, dictates the lifespan of stars, and even affects the passage of light. In its complex tapestry, the cosmos weaves a seamless narrative of unity and order, ensuring the celestial bodies move in harmonious synchronization. This cosmic choreography, so vital for the stability of the universe, is akin to the role communication plays in our team's journey.

Just as space-time connects the cosmos, communication is the invisible thread that binds our team, harmonizing our efforts, synchronizing our actions. It is through communication that we share our ideas, voice our concerns, express our aspirations, and chart our path forward. It serves as our very own space-time fabric, keeping us united and aligned in our quest for Galactic Excellence.

To harness the power of communication, we must first appreciate its dual nature - speaking and listening. When we speak, we launch our thoughts, like comets, into the collective mind-space of our team, seeding ideas, stimulating thought, and inspiring action. However, speaking is but one side of the cosmic coin. Listening, the art of receiving and understanding others' ideas, is equally crucial. When we listen, we open our minds to new perspectives, widen our horizons, and truly appreciate the diverse constellation of thoughts that our team represents.

In this dance of speaking and listening, we nurture a sense of mutual respect and understanding. Like celestial bodies moving in perfect harmony, our individual energies and talents align towards our common goals. As we navigate the nebulae of challenges and cross the event horizons of difficulties, this synchrony fuels our shared mission, propelling us towards the distant galaxies of success.

Remember, Star Seeker, in the vast universe of teamwork and leadership, communication is our space-time fabric. It is the element that unifies, the force that synchronizes, and the art that, when mastered, brings us a step closer to our coveted Galactic Excellence. Let us cherish this art and weave a shared story of success in the cosmic tapestry of our quest.

〈 〉

The Gravity of Influence: Leadership in the Cosmos

Just as the cosmos is bound together by the invisible yet undeniably potent force of gravity, teams are united by a similar force - the dynamic power of leadership. Consider, for a moment, the vast celestial landscape. Stars, planets, asteroids, and even rogue comets, all held in an intricate cosmic ballet by the inescapable pull of gravity. Such is the essence of leadership within a team. Like gravity, it is the leader's influence that provides direction, maintains unity, and ensures that each member orbits the shared objective of our mission: Galactic Excellence.

A leader, much like a celestial body exerting gravitational influence, has the ability to draw the team towards a common goal. Their vision becomes the guiding star, their determination the fuel, and their actions the thrusters that propel the team forward. A leader's words can motivate like the fiery outburst of a supernova, their decisions can redirect trajectories like gravitational slingshots, and their steadfast commitment can provide the stability of a predictable orbit.

But be aware, Star Seeker, that leadership is not merely about pulling along. The gravitational pull of a celestial body is in constant interaction with the motion of those around it - a delicate dance of push and pull. Similarly, true leadership involves understanding the individual energies, motivations, and talents of team members. It is about guiding, not dictating; inspiring, not commanding. Just as celestial bodies move in harmony under the guidance of gravity, a team moves toward its goal under the influence of compassionate and understanding leadership.

Each one of you is a leader, a celestial body with the potential to exert your own gravity of influence. As we embark on this cosmic voyage towards Galactic Excellence, remember that leadership is an opportunity, a responsibility, and a journey. And, just as gravity is essential for the celestial order, your leadership is critical in our quest.

Hold fast to your gravitational power, let it guide and inspire your fellow Star Seekers. Lead with empathy, vision, and resilience. In the vast cosmos of teamwork and leadership, let your gravitational influence bring us all closer to our shared ambition, our stellar mission - the pursuit of Galactic Excellence.

《 》

Quantum Resonance: Building a Harmonious Team

In the mysterious realm of quantum physics, there is a phenomenon known as 'quantum resonance'—when particles vibrate in harmony, their energies align and resonate, creating a beautifully synchronized dance of matter. This serves as a fitting metaphor for the harmony we strive for within our team in our grand pursuit of Galactic Excellence.

Creating a harmonious team is like tuning into a universal frequency where everyone's individual energies combine to create a powerful, unified field. It's a process that requires shared goals, mutual respect, and a supportive environment.

Imagine a symphony of stars. Each one unique, each one essential, all contributing to the magnificent orchestration of the night sky. This is the epitome of a harmonious team - diverse yet united, unique yet collaborative. The objective is not to become identical entities but to create an intricate cosmic melody where every note, every star, and every team member has a part to play.

The path to building such a team begins with shared goals. Just as constellations are bound by invisible lines creating meaningful patterns, a team must be linked by common objectives. A shared purpose ignites the same fire in every heart, aligning energies and encouraging collective strides towards Galactic Excellence.

Mutual respect, like the unfaltering laws of physics governing our cosmos, is the foundation upon which this celestial symphony is built. Appreciate the unique light each star—each team member—brings to the constellation. Understand the strengths, acknowledge the challenges, and honor the journey. This respect fuels the resonance, allowing the team to vibrate harmoniously in their cosmic dance.

Lastly, nurturing a supportive environment allows the symphony to flourish. In the same way a nebula provides the right conditions for stars to form, a supportive environment enables team members to grow. It fosters open communication, encourages creative risk-taking, and provides a safe space for growth. It is within this environment that individuals transform into team members, stars align into constellations, and goals morph into achievements.

In the quest for Galactic Excellence, harmony is not a mere luxury, but a necessity. A harmonious team creates the potential for extraordinary achievements in our cosmic voyage. Let's tune into that quantum frequency together, let's build our symphony of stars, and let's set the cosmos ablaze with our harmonious pursuit of Galactic Excellence.

⟨ ⟩

Interstellar Impact: The Power of Shared Success

In our quest for Galactic Excellence, we discover that each of us, much like the individual stars in a galaxy, radiates a distinct light. Each achievement, every success, no matter how seemingly insignificant, contributes to the grand illumination of the cosmic journey we undertake together.

Just as a single star's light influences the collective glow of its galaxy, each team member's triumph adds to the overall success of the team. This ripple effect, this Interstellar Impact, beautifully mirrors the interconnectedness of our universe.

Consider the cosmic dance of a galaxy. Even the faintest star contributes its light, adding to the magnificent spiral of brilliance we admire from afar. In isolation, the light of that single star might go unnoticed, lost amidst the vast darkness of the cosmos. But in the celestial choir of the galaxy, it becomes indispensable.

So it is with individual success within a team. Each achievement, every innovation, no matter how small, sends waves of positive impact that ripple through the team, inspiring others, boosting morale, and contributing to the cumulative success. It's a celebration of collective achievement that results from the sum of individual victories.

Understanding this dynamic is essential on our journey. It eradicates the shadow of competition, replacing it with the glow of cooperation. It encourages us to cheer each other on, knowing that a win for one is a win for all. It fosters a culture of shared success, where every accomplishment is celebrated and every individual feels valued.

We are bound together by our shared mission. We're entangled in our pursuit of Galactic Excellence, and each victory propels us forward, lighting the path for others to follow.

Take a moment to appreciate the collective brilliance of your team. Celebrate every win, no matter how small, and see how it adds to the collective glow. Recognize that each success is a valuable sparkle of stardust that adds to your cosmic journey.

Remember, in our shared quest, no achievement is insignificant, no success too small. Each contributes to our Interstellar Impact, propelling us closer to our shared vision of Galactic Excellence. As we journey together through the cosmos, let's celebrate our shared success, let's value our unique contributions, and let's light up the universe with our collective brilliance.

《 》

Wormhole Wisdom: Learning from Each Other

Every entity in the universe, from the tiniest particle to the grandest galaxy, holds a story, a lesson that can inform our journey. Similarly, each Star Seeker within a team brings a wealth of experiences, insights, and skills that others can learn from. In this vibrant pool of shared wisdom, we find the echoes of the universe's wisdom – the Wormhole Wisdom.

Wormholes in the cosmos are mysterious and fascinating entities. They bridge two separate points in space-time, creating a shortcut, a direct path to traverse vast cosmic distances. Imagine if we could utilize such a construct in our pursuit of knowledge and skills within our team! That's precisely the function our team's shared wisdom serves.

When we share experiences, teach skills, or discuss ideas, we essentially create cognitive wormholes that bridge our distinct islands of knowledge. These wormholes allow for swift, direct transfer of wisdom, saving us from lengthy voyages of discovery that we would otherwise need to undertake individually.

Just as a celestial traveler would utilize a wormhole to quickly traverse the cosmos, a Star Seeker can take advantage of the shared wisdom within the team to expedite their learning process. This exchange is not a one-way journey; it's an interstellar freeway of reciprocal enlightenment. By sharing and learning from each other, we shorten the path to knowledge, speeding up our quest for Galactic Excellence.

So, fellow Star Seekers, let's create these wormholes within our team. Ask questions, share your experiences, teach a skill you've mastered. Do not hoard your wisdom; instead, let it illuminate the path for others. Every nugget of wisdom you share and every insight you gain from others helps create a web of cognitive wormholes, enabling swift and effective learning.

In this united field of teamwork and leadership, we're not isolated celestial bodies. We're entangled entities, bound together in our quest for knowledge and excellence. Remember, every interaction is an opportunity to learn, every conversation a chance to share wisdom.

Cherish this Wormhole Wisdom, Star Seeker. Harness it, nurture it, and let it guide you and your team in your noble pursuit of Galactic Excellence. Together, you can traverse the vast cosmos of knowledge at warp speed, every journey enriched by the shared wisdom and unique insights of your fellow travelers.

《 》

Cosmic Leadership: Leading in the Vast Unknown

Stepping into the unknown, whether it be the boundless expanse of space or the uncharted realm of a novel project, is an exhilarating yet daunting prospect. Just like the celestial navigators of yore, leaders often find themselves at the helm of their starship, gazing into the vast unknown. It is here that Cosmic Leadership truly shines.

In the cosmos, black holes, supernovae, dark matter, and countless other unknown entities lay hidden in the void, waiting to be discovered. Similarly, leaders encounter unforeseen challenges, unexpected setbacks, and untapped potential. Embracing these uncertainties and navigating them with grace and confidence is the hallmark of a Cosmic Leader.

A Cosmic Leader understands that the unknown is not something to fear but to welcome. It is in the crucible of the unfamiliar that the most profound discoveries are made, the most significant growth achieved. They harness the uncertainty, transforming it into a propellant, thrusting their team toward Galactic Excellence.

But how does one become a Cosmic Leader? What celestial tools should they have in their arsenal?

Firstly, just as a celestial navigator trusts their astrolabe and compass, a Cosmic Leader trusts their instincts and knowledge. They are grounded in their expertise yet remain open-minded, embracing new ideas and perspectives.

Secondly, they exhibit the courage of explorers venturing into unexplored territories. A Cosmic Leader bravely charts a course into the unknown, instilling confidence and inspiring their team to follow suit. They understand that great rewards often require risks and that the path to Galactic Excellence is seldom a well-trodden trail.

Finally, the Cosmic Leader is agile and adaptable. Just as the cosmos is in a constant state of flux, the landscape of our projects and goals often change. A Cosmic Leader, much like a skilled helmsman, swiftly adjusts their course to align with these changes, ensuring their team remains on the path to success.

Leading in the vast unknown can be daunting, Star Seeker, but remember, it is also a source of boundless potential. Embrace it, harness it, and let it propel you towards Galactic Excellence. For it is the leaders who dare to venture into the unknown, who chart their course among the stars, that truly embody the spirit of a Cosmic Leader. Be that leader, Star Seeker. Navigate the vast unknown with courage, agility, and unwavering resolve, and let your Cosmic Leadership guide your team to stellar heights.

《 》

Quantum Entanglement – A Cosmic Dance of Synergy

As our voyage through this cosmic chapter draws to an end, we arrive at a profound realization, akin to a grand cosmic revelation. Just as quantum particles across the universe are interconnected, so too are the concepts of teamwork and leadership in our journey towards Galactic Excellence. They are entwined, each feeding into and shaping the other in an exquisite symphony of synergy.

In our quest for excellence, it is vital to understand and embrace this Quantum Entanglement. The gravity of our influence as leaders pulls our team towards shared goals, while our team, in turn, shapes us as leaders helping us navigate the unknown territories of our mission. It's a cyclical, dynamic process – a dance that transcends the boundaries of individuals and uplifts the collective towards a shared vision.

But remember, Star Seeker, while we may draw inspiration from the stars, this is not a solitary journey. Our paths are intertwined, our destinies interconnected. Every conversation, every shared success, every moment of learning from one another, adds to this quantum dance, making it richer and more vibrant.

Embrace your role in this dance. Whether you are a leader guiding your team through uncharted territories, or a team member contributing your unique skills and perspectives, know that you are an integral part of this cosmic ballet. Your thoughts, actions, and decisions, no matter how small, have ripples throughout your team, shaping and guiding it in ways you may not even realize.

Never forget, Star Seeker, we are all dancing together in this cosmic dance. Each of us is a vital part of the grand symphony of the universe. So, embrace the dance. The stage is set, the cosmos is waiting. The journey towards Galactic Excellence continues... together.

Chapter 8: Neutron Star Strength - The Resilience of the Cosmic Warrior

Neutron Stars – Cosmic Symbols of Resilience

These celestial bodies are stellar remnants of colossal supernova explosions, blazing brightly against the darkness of the cosmos. Just like these astral entities, each one of us is a bright beacon of resilience, capable of withstanding the most formidable of adversities in our mission towards Galactic Excellence.

Resilience, in its purest form, is our capacity to bounce back from life's supernovas. It's our ability to keep our starships afloat amid the turbulences of cosmic storms. The universe throws at us asteroid showers of problems and challenges, but it's our resilience that helps us steer clear of destructive paths and venture forth, stronger and more determined.

Now, think of neutron stars, those extraordinary wonders. Born out of cataclysmic events, they endure, emitting beams of radiation across the universe, continuing to shine long after their parent stars have faded into obscurity. In many ways, aren't we, the Star Seekers, very much akin to these neutron stars? Our resilience is what allows us to emerge stronger from life's supernovas, illuminating our paths and inspiring others in our pursuit of Galactic Excellence.

So, let's embark on this journey of discovering the neutron star within us. Let's explore the untapped reserves of strength that reside in our inner cosmos. This chapter will serve as your star map, guiding you through the fascinating world of resilience – the Neutron Star Strength. As we voyage together through these pages, may you find inspiration in the resilience of neutron stars and learn to harness that power in your quest for Galactic Excellence.

⟨ ⟩

The Birth of a Neutron Star: The Formation of Resilience

Our journey continues as we delve deeper into the realm of resilience. These cosmic marvels are born out of cataclysmic supernovas, where parent stars, unable to resist the crushing force of their own gravity, explode, casting away their outer shells and leaving behind a compact core - a newborn neutron star.

Much like the birth of these resilient celestial objects, our own resilience forms in the crucible of trials and tribulations. Challenges are our personal supernovas, events that test our fortitude, threaten to tear us apart, only to leave behind a stronger, more resilient core. Just as a dying star's collapse births a neutron star, adversity is the birthplace of our resilience.

We are on a quest for Galactic Excellence. This journey is not always smooth; it is often dotted with black holes of setbacks and meteor showers of disappointments. These hurdles may threaten to throw us off course, to derail our journey. But remember, each challenge is an opportunity to forge our resilience, to become our own version of a neutron star.

Consider the hurdles you have encountered on your quest. Reflect on the asteroid showers of setbacks you've endured, the black holes of failures you've emerged from. Each of these challenges was a supernova event in your journey. And what did you do? You bounced back, you endured, and emerged stronger - you turned into a neutron star.

Resilience is not something we are born with; it is something we develop, something we forge in the depths of adversity. Like a neutron star forming amidst cosmic chaos, our resilience is a testament to our ability to endure and shine brightly in the face of adversity.

So, whenever you find yourself in the midst of a personal supernova, remember the birth of a neutron star. Stand firm, brace for impact, and remember that this challenge will only forge you into a stronger, more resilient Star Seeker. And remember, after the supernova comes the shining, resilient neutron star – your Neutron Star Strength.

❰ ❱

Supernova Survivor: Standing Strong Amidst Adversity

As we chart our course deeper into the cosmic realm of resilience, let's shift our gaze to an awe-inspiring spectacle – a supernova. The explosion that births a neutron star is not a gentle process. It is a violent eruption, a radiant release of energy that shatters the starry silence of the cosmos.

Star Seeker, we often find ourselves in the throes of our personal supernovas. These are the times when life's challenges explode around us in a dazzling display of overwhelming emotions, unexpected obstacles, and daunting doubts.

Picture this: You're a neutron star at the heart of a supernova. Around you, adversity detonates, threatening to consume you, to tear you apart. It feels overwhelming, it feels impossible. But you, the heart of this celestial storm, stand firm. You embrace the explosive energy, channel it, and use it to forge yourself into an emblem of endurance. You are the supernova survivor.

Resilience is this very survival amidst adversity. It is the ability to face life's supernovas, to endure its heat, and emerge as a shining testament of cosmic strength. Resilience is the neutron star that shines bright even after the most cataclysmic explosions.

There is a potent lesson we can take from the survival of a neutron star: it is the transformative power of resilience. It is our protective shell in the face of adversity, our guiding light in the darkest cosmos, and our unwavering strength amidst the most challenging supernovas.

Remember, your journey towards Galactic Excellence will be marked with supernovas of various magnitudes. These are your battles, your challenges. Embrace them, endure them, and let them forge you into a supernova survivor. You are not merely facing adversity; you are harnessing it, transforming it into resilience, into your very own Neutron Star Strength.

《 》

The Pulsar's Pulse: Maintaining Momentum

Have you ever gazed at a pulsar, Star Seekers? These neutron stars spin at breathtaking speeds, emitting beams of electromagnetic radiation. Their pulse, consistent and unwavering, paints a cosmic rhythm across the universe. They are the celestial epitome of constant momentum, a fitting symbol for the resilience we aim to master on our journey to Galactic Excellence.

Like pulsars, we too spin in the universe of our lives, facing challenges and obstacles that seek to slow our rotation. They come in many forms - unforeseen circumstances, personal setbacks, or even the gravitational pull of self-doubt. Yet, just as a pulsar maintains its spin, so must we maintain our momentum.

Resilience is not merely surviving adversity. It is about maintaining forward motion, keeping your pulse steady, and not letting the spin of life slow down. It's about finding the strength to keep turning, keep moving, keep progressing, even when the cosmos seems to conspire against you.

Think of each obstacle as a cosmic force acting upon your spin. It might jolt you, perhaps even wobble you, but your pulsar's pulse, your momentum, should remain undeterred. Let the rhythm of resilience beat within you. Each pulsation is a testament to your strength, an echo of your perseverance, a step towards your goal. It is the hum of progress, the constant rotation towards your dreams.

Remember, Star Seekers, the neutron star does not stop spinning after the supernova, and neither should you. Every rotation, every beat of your pulsar's pulse, is a testament to your resilience, your capacity to maintain momentum in the face of adversity. Embrace your Pulsar's Pulse. It is the rhythm of your journey, the tempo of your resilience, the heartbeat of your pursuit of Galactic Excellence. The pulsar in you is the rhythm of resilience. Dance to its cosmic beat. Keep spinning, keep pulsating, keep moving forward, for in every pulse lies the strength of a Neutron Star.

〈 〉

The Neutron Star's Density: Building Emotional Fortitude

Just like the density of a neutron star, emotional fortitude is about the concentration of your emotional energy, your capacity to withstand and bounce back from life's pressures without losing your core integrity. It is about your ability to carry the weight of your emotions, just as a neutron star carries its immense density, without succumbing to the forces that threaten to tear you apart.

How, you might ask, does one go about building such formidable emotional fortitude? The process is both a journey and a practice.

Begin by acknowledging your emotions as integral to your journey, not as obstacles but as indicators of your personal growth. Emotions are not weaknesses; they are a testament to our humanity, to our capacity for empathy, passion, and connection. Like the density of a neutron star, they contribute to our strength.

Next, practice emotional awareness. Learn to identify and understand your emotions. Embrace them, sit with them, learn from them. This will help you develop emotional agility, the ability to navigate through your emotions with grace and wisdom, just as a neutron star navigates the cosmic seas with its incredible density.

Finally, foster self-compassion. Be gentle with yourself as you experience the flux of emotions. Allow yourself to feel without judgment or criticism. Remember, every neutron star began as a star that dared to collapse under its weight. Your struggles and your emotional burdens are not signs of failure; they are proof of your courage to experience life in its entirety.

Developing the density of emotional fortitude is a continuous process, one that requires patience, understanding, and plenty of self-love. It's not about suppressing or ignoring your emotions but learning to carry them with grace, strength, and resilience. Like the neutron star, we can each build a core of emotional resilience that is as dense and as unyielding as the cosmos itself.

《 》

Gravitational Waves: The Ripple Effects of Resilience

Gravitational waves, invisible yet potent, ripple out from a neutron star, subtly influencing its celestial surroundings. In a similar vein, the impact of our resilience extends far beyond the boundaries of our personal being, impacting those around us in ways we may not immediately perceive.

In this sense, resilience is not a solitary journey. It extends into our relationships, our communities, our workplaces. When we face adversity with strength, when we rebound from setbacks with an unwavering spirit, we are not only fueling our individual journey towards Galactic Excellence, but we are also lighting the path for others. We are sending out gravitational waves of courage, strength, and determination that can inspire those around us.

In a world that often feels heavy with challenges and setbacks, the power of your resilience can provide the hope that others need to keep going. It can foster a sense of collective resilience, a shared strength that binds us together, making us all stronger in the face of adversity.

Take a moment to recognize and honor this impact. Every time you rise, every time you dare to keep going despite the challenges—you are sending out powerful waves into your universe. You are making a difference.

So, let your resilience ripple outward, touching and inspiring others. May your journey towards Galactic Excellence not only be a testament to your personal strength but also serve as a beacon of hope, encouraging others to discover and embrace their own cosmic warrior spirit. Together, we will ride these waves, drawing strength from each other, as we journey onwards to a universe where resilience reigns supreme.

In this cosmic dance of resilience, you are not just a participant, but a pivot point, a beacon of hope and strength. As we conclude this chapter, I invite you to delve deeper, to seek your own resilient core, and to embrace the Neutron Star Strength within you. The path to Galactic Excellence is strewn with adversities, but armed with resilience, no obstacle is insurmountable.

⟪ ⟫

The Neutron Star Within – Unleashing Your Inner Resilience

As our cosmic voyage in this chapter reaches its end, it becomes ever more apparent how profoundly resilience underpins the journey towards Galactic Excellence. The testament of the neutron star's indomitable strength serves as a beacon of inspiration, illuminating the path to our own potential resilience.

Each challenge we encounter, each setback we face, each difficult situation we navigate is a cosmic crucible, shaping and strengthening our resilience. It's an opportunity for us to access the neutron star within us – that dense core of inner strength and emotional fortitude that allows us to bounce back and continue our journey.

As Star Seekers, we have the power to send ripples of resilience across our own personal cosmos, just as a neutron star does in the vast universe. Our endurance can touch the lives of others, encouraging them to discover their own resilience and furthering our collective quest for Galactic Excellence.

Unleashing your inner resilience, your Neutron Star Strength, is not a one-time event. It's an ongoing process, a relentless forging of will and spirit akin to the ceaseless spinning of a neutron star. And remember, the ripple effect of your resilience, much like the neutron star's gravitational waves, extends far beyond what you may perceive in the moment.

In this cosmic dance of resilience, you are not just a participant, but a pivot point, a beacon of hope and strength. As we conclude this chapter, I invite you to delve deeper, to seek your own resilient core, and to embrace the Neutron Star Strength within you. The path to Galactic Excellence is strewn with adversities, but armed with resilience, no obstacle is insurmountable.

With each revolution, let us spin stronger and shine brighter. For in the heart of resilience, there is an indomitable spirit, a neutron star waiting to illuminate the path to Galactic Excellence.

Chapter 9: Pulsar's Pulse - The Steady Heartbeat of Consistency and Momentum

Pulsar's Pulse - The Heartbeat of the Cosmos

In the quiet hum of the cosmos a pulsar beats. Its rhythmic pulses sweep across the galaxy, a heartbeat echoing through the vast silence of space. A pulsar is a star, a cosmic sun, born from the spectacular death throes of another larger star. And yet, it lives, thrums, endures with a steady unerring regularity that permeates the interstellar expanse. It's in this steadfast pulse that we find a compelling embodiment of an essential quality in our pursuit of Galactic Excellence—cosmic consistency.

Consistency, much like the pulsar's heartbeat, is an often-understated yet profound determinant of success. The pulsar, with its rhythmic light and radio wave beams, appears to blink like a twinkling star symbolizing a sun that acts as a lighthouse amid the ocean. Its beacon, however, is unwavering, a testament to the star's unyielding rotation.

Much like this celestial lighthouse, each of us has a mission, a journey, a pursuit—our very own True North Star towards which we navigate. The route to this star, paved with dreams, ambitions, and the very essence of our potential, is a journey best undertaken with the metronome of consistency ticking steadily within us.

Yet, in a world of quick fixes and instant gratification, the concept of consistency—steady, patient, and relentless—can be undervalued, even forgotten. This chapter seeks to resurface the profound impact of the pulsar's pulse in our journey to Galactic Excellence. It serves to illuminate the immense strength inherent in maintaining a constant pace, in moving forward with unyielding resolve no matter how formidable the obstacles that lie in our path.

So, let's uncover the secrets nestled within its unceasing rhythm and explore how to harness this interstellar strength in our journey. After all, within each of us there exists a pulsar, a steady drum that pulses with resilience, courage, and the power of consistency. It's time to listen, to feel its rhythm, and to let it guide us towards our True North Star.

⟨ ⟩

The Cosmic Metronome: Understanding the Power of Consistency

In the cosmos, a pulsar is a cosmic metronome maintaining a steady rhythm amidst the chaos of interstellar space. It's an unyielding celestial body that, despite its explosive birth and turbulent existence, offers a rhythmic regularity that stands as a testament to the power of consistency. Like this distant star, we too are called to discover and nurture the rhythm of persistence in pursuit of our True North Star.

In our earthly journey towards Galactic Excellence, consistency operates as an invisible but vital driving force. It may not have the dramatic flair of sudden breakthroughs or the immediate satisfaction of quick wins, but consistency wields a quiet power that gradually shapes our trajectory, much like the gentle but relentless shaping of a river carving a canyon.

It's important to note that being consistent is not about maintaining an unchanging state. Rather, it is about embracing a dedicated rhythm of growth and adaptation in response to changing circumstances, much like a pulsar maintains its pulse while orbiting in the gravitational dance of the cosmos.

The essence of consistency lies in taking small, repeated actions, consistently done well over time. These seemingly insignificant acts, when performed with consistency, compound into monumental results. They are the stepping stones that bridge the gap between where we are and where we aspire to be.

Consider the learning of a new language or a musical instrument. No one masters these skills in a day or even a month. They require the regular, disciplined practice of scales, of phrases, of tones. It is the continual dedication to improvement, the consistent action over time, that transforms the novice into the virtuoso.

So too, in our quest for Galactic Excellence, we find our growth and progress hinged upon this very principle. The development of our talents, the realization of our dreams, the achievement of our goals - they all spring from the fertile ground of consistent action.

However, embracing the power of consistency is not without its challenges. Life, much like the universe itself, is a dynamic and ever-evolving entity. We face obstacles, unexpected twists and turns that could deter us from our set course. But it is precisely in these moments that we must call upon our inner pulsar, to maintain our pulse, our rhythm, in the face of adversity.

And so, as we journey further into the mysteries of the pulsar's heartbeat, let us delve deeper into understanding how to cultivate this cosmic metronome within us, embracing the power of consistency as we chart our course towards our very own Galactic Excellence.

《 》

The Pulsar's Spin: The Art of Maintaining Momentum

Within the ever spinning of the cosmos, a pulsar keeps its rhythm. In the face of cosmic forces that continually strive to slow its spin, this celestial titan preserves its pace, demonstrating an unparalleled art of maintaining momentum. The pulsar, through its unwavering spin, imparts a significant lesson for us on our journey towards Galactic Excellence: the importance of sustaining momentum, no matter the forces that seek to deter us.

Our momentum is similar to the pulsar's galactic heartbeat that ceaselessly emits beams of light as it spins, we too radiate our greatest potential when we maintain our rhythmic momentum. It's important to understand that the journey to our True North Star is not a sprint, but a marathon — a long-haul voyage through time and space where preserving our cosmic momentum is key.

In this celestial dance of life, momentum is our friend. Once gained, it propels us forward, eases the journey and fuels our resolve. It's the inertia that transforms a decision into action, an action into habit, and a habit into character. But, much like in the cosmos, there are forces at play in our lives that resist this momentum — forces like fear, self-doubt, and complacency.

In the face of these resistive forces, how do we, like the pulsar, maintain our spin? The secret lies in the pulsar's nature itself — cosmic consistency. As we discovered earlier, consistency is not about rigid inflexibility but about maintaining a rhythm of steady progress, a continuous pulsation of actions aligned with our True North Star.

It means committing to the journey, no matter how challenging the path or tempting the shortcuts. It's about turning up, day in and day out, whether the stars align or not. It's about small, steady actions, pulsating with perseverance, determination, and unwavering commitment.

Maintaining momentum is also about adapting to change, much like a pulsar navigates the cosmic currents while keeping its rhythmic spin. We are called to be flexible in our approach, tweaking our trajectory when necessary, while remaining steadfastly devoted to our overall direction.

Moreover, the art of maintaining momentum involves celebrating progress, no matter how small. Each pulsation, each turn, each action that brings us closer to our goal is a victory worth recognizing. These small wins serve to refuel our momentum, reaffirming our direction and rekindling our resolve.

《 》

The Magnetic Field: Attracting Success with Consistency

As we continue our voyage, let us now turn our gaze to another unique characteristic of the pulsar – its powerful magnetic field. The pulsar's magnetic field is incredibly potent, so much so that it is capable of ripping apart atoms and emitting intense beams of radiation. This magnetic field acts as the pulsar's heart, beating with every spin and defining its very essence.

Much like the magnetic field of a pulsar, consistency in our pursuits has an attractive force of its own. With consistency, we create a magnetic field around us that pulls our dreams closer, transforms our aspirations into reality, and attracts success.

Consistency is not just about repetitive action; it's about sustained, aligned, and focused effort towards our True North Star. It's this kind of effort that sends a powerful signal out into the universe, a beacon of commitment and resolve that begins to pull our desired outcomes towards us. It's the steadfast pulsation of action that creates a rhythm of success.

This magnetic effect of consistency can be seen in every sphere of life. It's the athlete, practicing every day, rain or shine, whose consistent effort magnetizes gold medals and championship trophies. It's the artist, creating relentlessly, whose consistent craft pulls in recognition and acclaim. It's the entrepreneur, iterating and improving day by day, whose steadfast dedication attracts business growth and success. The stories may vary, but the common thread is the magnetic power of consistency.

However, attracting success isn't just about consistency in action. It's also about consistency in thought, belief, and attitude. Our mental and emotional state influences the strength and direction of our magnetic field. A consistent, positive mindset acts as a potent magnet, aligning our energies and actions towards our desired outcomes.

When we believe in our potential, commit to our growth, and trust in our journey, we create a powerful mental magnet that attracts opportunities, resources, and the right people into our lives. A pulsar's magnetic field is an inherent part of its identity, just as our mindset should be an integral part of ours. To truly magnetize success, we must maintain a steady pulse of optimism, resilience, and self-belief.

⟨ ⟩

Riding the Radio Waves: Transmitting Consistent Efforts

One of the most distinctive features of a pulsar is its powerful radio waves, radiating out into the cosmos like a cosmic lighthouse. These waves are generated by the pulsar's fast-spinning magnetic field, transforming its energy into signals that can traverse immense distances in space. This unstoppable, rhythmic transmission has allowed us to discover and understand these fascinating celestial bodies, even from millions of light years away.

This phenomenon mirrors the ripple effect of our consistent actions. Just as the pulsar's radio waves reverberate across the vast cosmic expanse, our consistent efforts ripple out, influencing not just our immediate circumstances but also our broader journey towards Galactic Excellence.

Every action, no matter how small it may seem, transmits energy into the world around us. These signals, much like the pulsar's radio waves, have the power to cross boundaries, break barriers, and catalyze change. Each step we take, every task we complete, and every goal we meet sends out a wave of influence that alters our trajectory and impacts our environment.

For instance, consider the consistent efforts of a dedicated musician, diligently practicing scales and harmonies every day. These seemingly small, repetitive actions send out waves of commitment and passion, influencing their future performances, their audience's reactions, and even the broader cultural landscape. Their daily dedication is the pulse, and the resulting music, appreciation, and impact are the far-reaching radio waves.

Consistency is more than just a personal practice; it's a powerful transmitter that amplifies our presence, communicates our commitment, and shapes our destiny. It tells the universe, "I am here. I am persistent. I am unwavering in my journey."

This ripple effect of consistent actions isn't limited to individual pursuits. It can permeate every corner of our lives impacting our personal growth, professional development, and interpersonal relationships. A steady pulse of kind words can strengthen a friendship, while a consistent commitment to learning can expand our professional opportunities.

As North Star Seekers, essentially beacons of powerful transmissions, we must remember that our actions, thoughts, and words are never isolated events. They are radio waves, broadcasting our presence and purpose in the universe. So, let's reflect the behavior of the pulsar and maintain our consistent efforts. For in doing so, we don't just move forward on our own path - we send powerful waves of influence that can resonate through the cosmos and echo into eternity.

⟨ ⟩

Neutron Star to Pulsar: Transformation through Persistence

The journey from a neutron star to a pulsar is a celestial marvel that encapsulates the transformative power of persistence and consistency. Born from the explosive remnants of a supernova, a neutron star may spin and emit beams of electromagnetic radiation, thus transforming into a pulsar - an emblem of steadfast rhythm echoing throughout the cosmos. This journey is not immediate, nor is it effortless; it is the result of enduring forces and unyielding persistence.

Much like a pulsar's journey, our path to Galactic Excellence is not a sprint but a marathon. It is a process that calls for consistent action, relentless dedication, and unyielding resilience. We, too, are shaped by our reactions to the supernovas in our lives, the explosive challenges that force us to evolve and grow.

We start our journey full of potential and kinetic energy. The changes are subtle at first, almost imperceptible. But with every action, with every spin, we send out signals of commitment and dedication. And gradually, with persistence, we transform into our own version of a pulsar - a beacon of consistent efforts, a testament to our resolve and endurance.

Consider an athlete training for a marathon. The transformation doesn't occur overnight. It's the product of weeks, months, and sometimes years of steady training - early morning runs, disciplined nutrition, and mental conditioning. The consistency of the routine, the relentless commitment to the process, transforms an individual into an athlete. It's their pulsar's pulse, their rhythm of consistency and momentum, which culminates in a transformative feat of endurance.

Or take the case of a writer. A novel, a masterpiece of literature, doesn't materialize at the snap of a finger. It's the fruit of countless hours of writing, researching, and editing. Each word, each sentence, and each chapter is a step in their consistent journey towards their goal. With every day's commitment to writing, they evolve, they transform from an individual with an idea to a celebrated author. Their pulsar's pulse is the rhythm of their keystrokes, a steady drum that narrates a tale of persistence and momentum.

And so, we must embrace the pulsar's pulse on our space voyage towards positive transformation. Whether we are spinning rapidly or slowly advancing, every revolution counts. Every pulse matters. We are all in our unique ways, cosmic warriors in the throes of transformation, gradually evolving through the power of persistence. Let's continue perusing our North Star with our pulsar's heartbeat as our anthem of Galactic Excellence.

《 》

L ighthouse of the Galaxy: Guiding Your Path with Your Heart

Pulsars, with their rhythmic emissions of light and radio waves, have earned the name 'Lighthouses of the Galaxy.' Their enduring pulses of energy cut through the cosmic darkness, providing reliable and consistent signals in an otherwise chaotic universe. These steadfast cosmic navigators provide us with a powerful metaphor on our galactic quest for excellence, demonstrating how the heartbeat of consistency can guide our path, much like a lighthouse guiding a ship through a dark night.

In pursuit of your True North Star, the destination may seem distant, the journey full of obstacles. There will be moments when your path is clear, and progress is apparent. But there will also be times when you'll feel lost, unsure of your direction amidst the uncertainties and challenges. It's during these moments that you must harness your will and tune into your inner pulsar, your consistent heartbeat of action and determination that will guide you through the darkest nights.

Consistency is the rhythmic momentum but your heart is the source of light that can truly illuminate your path, the reliable beacon that provides direction when you are lost in the ocean of possibilities. Consider the artist who crafts their skill daily, not just when inspiration strikes. They commit to pursue what's in their heart, supported by a rhythmic pulse of practice and critique that refines their craft, guiding them closer to their True North Star.

The entrepreneur, facing the uncertainty of the market, maintains a steady pulse of innovation and resilience, even when success is not immediately visible. Their consistency becomes their navigational checkpoint guiding them through setbacks until they reach their goal of creating something meaningful and valuable for their customers and family.

The student, navigating the vast universe of knowledge, holds fast to a consistent study routine. Each day they add to their knowledge, building on previous understanding. This routine, this steady pulse for the love of learning, becomes their guiding beacon, leading them towards academic excellence.

It is crucial to note that your heart, the core of your navigational system, not be erratic or haphazard. It needs to be focused, disciplined, and consistent. Similarly, your actions should not be sporadic or inconsistent. To guide you towards your True North Star, you need to be clear with a disciplined approach in your daily endeavors. Even the smallest consistent effort, when accumulated over time, can result in a significant impact.

In a universe filled with uncertainty, let the pulsar's heartbeat inspire you to stay consistent in your actions. Let your steady drum of pursuing your passions serve as a guiding light, cutting through the darkness of doubt and uncertainty, and leading you on the path to Galactic Excellence.

And remember, even when your path seems obscured by darkness, trust in your heart. Let it guide you, for it knows the way. It is your rhythmic beacon of persistence, your lighthouse in the galaxy, consistently leading you towards your True North Star.

Chapter 10: Voyage to an Exoplanet - Charting New Frontiers

Exoplanets – The New Frontiers of the Cosmos

As a north star seeker, you're no stranger to the allure of the uncharted, the unexplored, the new. For millennia, humans looked up at the stars, desiring to understand the unending darkness punctuated by the shimmering beacons of distant suns. That thirst for exploration, that sense of wonder, is what drove us to leave footprints on the moon and send rovers to Mars.

In the immensity of the cosmos, however, our journeys have only just begun. One of the most exhilarating new frontiers in this space age is the exploration of exoplanets, celestial bodies revolving around stars beyond our solar system. With the potential to harbor life or serve as future homes for humanity, exoplanets are a symbol of the unknown, beckoning us to discover their secrets.

But, as you gaze at the night sky, pondering these distant worlds, **consider this**: aren't we all, in our own way, explorers charting new frontiers? As we venture into the untouched landscapes of our personal growth or navigate the complex terrains of professional endeavors, we embark on an exploration akin to voyaging to an exoplanet. The journey may be daunting, filled with uncertainty and challenges. Yet, it is in confronting these unknowns that we find our true potential, unveiling layers of our character previously unseen.

《 》

C harting the Unknown: The Adventure of New Ideas

The cosmos invites us on a perpetual journey of discovery. As we probe the vast expanse of space, we're not just mapping out celestial bodies; we're exploring the limitless frontiers of our understanding, our capabilities, and our potential. And at the heart of this exploration lies the thrill of embracing the new, the undiscovered – new ideas that redefine our perspective and transform our path towards Galactic Excellence.

Consider for a moment, an astronaut setting foot on an uncharted exoplanet. The alien landscape stretches out, its unique topography whispering secrets waiting to be uncovered. This is no terrain for the faint-hearted, yet the explorer strides forward, buoyed by an insatiable curiosity, the exhilaration of discovery, and the potential of unearthing profound wisdom. Similarly, when we venture into the realm of new ideas, we become pioneers in our own right, daring to traverse the unfamiliar landscapes of thought and insight.

The exploration of new ideas is an adventure that goes beyond intellectual growth. It serves as a catalyst for our personal evolution, equipping us with fresh perspectives, novel strategies, and diverse skill sets. Embracing new ideas cultivates resilience, as we learn to adapt to unfamiliar concepts and situations. It fosters creativity, enabling us to imagine innovative solutions to challenges. Most importantly, it empowers us to shape our own journey, to mold our own path towards our True North Star.

Exploration is, by nature, a leap into the unknown, and it requires courage. But remember, Star Seeker, the universe rewards the brave. The exoplanet of a new idea may seem alien and intimidating from afar, but it is on these uncharted lands that we often find the most precious nuggets of wisdom, the most transformative insights, and the most profound growth. So, muster your courage, fuel your curiosity, and let us embark on this grand voyage of exploring new ideas together.

⟨ ⟩

The Exoplanet's Atmosphere: Nurturing an Environment for Novelty

It's not just the thrill of setting foot on an uncharted exoplanet that grips an explorer's heart; it's the potential of what that new world might harbor. Each exoplanet, with its unique atmosphere, offers the tantalizing possibility of life, of ecosystems vastly different from what we know. This novelty is at the heart of our exploration, a testament to the limitless creativity of the cosmos.

The same principle applies to our quest for Galactic Excellence. The atmosphere we foster – be it in our minds, our teams, or our communities – holds immense power in shaping the novelty and innovation we can bring forth. Like an exoplanet's atmosphere, which sets the stage for the emergence of life, a conducive environment can become the cradle for the birth and nurturing of new ideas.

Creating such an atmosphere requires us to embrace diversity in thought, to appreciate differing perspectives, and to cultivate an openness to change. It calls for us to foster a culture of curiosity, where questioning is encouraged and learning is celebrated. And above all, it demands us to cultivate a safe space for risk-taking, where fear of failure does not stifle innovation but propels it forward.

Star Seeker, remember that our minds are universes within themselves, teeming with countless ideas waiting to be discovered, just like exoplanets waiting to be explored. By nurturing an environment that encourages novelty, you are inviting yourself to break free from the shackles of the known and dare to chart the course of the unexplored.

So, let us venture forth into this cosmos of novelty. Like an exoplanet, let us create the right conditions for life – in this case, the life of fresh ideas and innovative solutions. Let's foster an atmosphere that encourages us to reach out, explore, and embrace the limitless potential of the universe within us.

《 》

G ravity Assist: Harnessing Existing Resources for Future Exploration

In the vast expanse of space, there's a fascinating concept that has facilitated the exploration of far-flung celestial bodies: the gravity assist, or gravitational slingshot. This maneuver involves a spacecraft using the gravity of a planet or another celestial body to alter its speed and trajectory, enabling it to reach distant destinations that would otherwise be beyond its capabilities. But what does this celestial maneuver have to do with our journey to Galactic Excellence? More than you might imagine, Star Seeker.

In the journey of exploring new ideas and frontiers, we often underestimate the power of our existing resources. Just as a spacecraft harnesses a planet's gravitational pull to catapult itself further into the cosmos, we can leverage our current knowledge, experiences, and resources to propel ourselves toward our True North Star.

Think about the wealth of experiences you've accumulated over the years. Each of these experiences, be they victories or setbacks, have the potential to serve as a gravity assist in your journey. They hold valuable lessons that can shape your trajectory, provide momentum, and aid in the exploration of new ideas.

Your existing knowledge, too, plays a crucial role. The expertise you've garnered, the skills you've honed, and the wisdom you've accumulated are invaluable resources. They form the basis from which you can branch out, a strong gravitational field from which you can launch your voyage into the unknown.

Furthermore, consider the people in your orbit – your mentors, colleagues, friends, and family. Their support, advice, and companionship can provide a powerful gravity assist, guiding you, challenging you, and assisting you in reaching your distant exoplanet of innovative ideas.

Remember, Star Seeker, while the allure of new frontiers is undeniable, don't neglect the resources that lie within your grasp. Just as a spacecraft performs a gravity assist to propel itself deeper into the cosmos, use your past experiences, your hard-earned knowledge, and your personal network as a gravitational force to propel you further in your exploration.

Harness these resources and allow them to boost your trajectory as you chart your path. The cosmos is vast, but with the gravity assist of your existing resources, no exoplanet – no idea or goal – is out of reach. Your journey to Galactic Excellence continues, and this gravity assist is here to speed you on your way.

Chapter 11: The Celestial Mirror - Reflecting On Self-Growth

The Celestial Mirror - Reflections of the Self

Let us imagine, for a moment, that each of us has our very own celestial mirror, a unique, personal cosmos reflected in its surface. This mirror allows us to look inward, to study the expanse of our inner universe as we would the space above. It enables us to examine the galaxies of our strengths, the constellations of our talents, the nebulae of our dreams, and the black holes of our fears and insecurities.

In this chapter, we shall turn our telescopes inward and begin our exploration of this personal celestial mirror. A mission that may appear daunting initially but holds the promise of guiding us toward a more profound understanding of our own selves.

Just as astronomers study the cosmos to unravel the mysteries of the universe, we too shall delve into introspection, a practice as essential to our journey to Galactic Excellence as stargazing is to an astronomer. By learning to study our reflections in our celestial mirrors, we equip ourselves with the tools needed to navigate the universe of our personal and professional lives more effectively.

《 》

The Reflective Surface: Embracing Self-Observation

In our celestial mirror, each star, each planet, each nebula represents facets of our selves, of our character, and of our potentials. To seek Galactic Excellence, we must first become astronomers of our inner universe, observing ourselves with curiosity and compassion, illuminating the hidden corners of our character, our emotions, our motivations, and our dreams.

You see, the process of self-observation is not unlike gazing upon the cosmos through a telescope. Each observation, each thought and feeling, each action and reaction, is a star in our personal universe. Some shine brightly, drawing our attention with their spectacular luminosity. These could be our strengths, our successes, our joys.

Others might be dimmer, tucked away in the far-off corners of our internal galaxy. These could be our weaknesses, our challenges, our fears. Like distant celestial bodies, they might be harder to observe, but they hold valuable insights, nonetheless.

When astronomers look into the cosmos, do they ignore the darkness between the stars, the mysteries of the black holes, or the obscurity of distant galaxies? No. They study these with equal interest, for they understand that each aspect of the cosmos, be it a radiant star or a mysterious black hole, contributes to the wholeness of the universe.

Likewise, in our journey of self-observation, we should not shy away from our challenges or fear our weaknesses. Instead, we should embrace them, study them, for they too are part of our universe. They offer us the opportunities for growth, the chance to turn weaknesses into strengths, fear into courage, and challenges into achievements.

So, take a moment. Pause. Look into your celestial mirror. Observe the constellation of your qualities, the galaxies of your thoughts, and the black holes of your fears. Acknowledge them, learn from them, and utilize this knowledge to navigate your path toward Galactic

Excellence. In the vast expanse of your inner cosmos, every star, every planet, every nebula, and even every black hole, matters.

《 》

Through the Looking Glass: Uncovering Hidden Aspects

Perhaps you've discovered a cluster of stars—talents or abilities—that you weren't aware you possessed. Maybe you've uncovered a nebula, a birthplace of new stars, signifying emerging interests or passions that could fuel your journey towards Galactic Excellence. Or you might even have come across a black hole, a void filled with fears or insecurities, demanding your attention and understanding.

Just like a celestial body hidden in the vast cosmos, these aspects of ourselves might have remained concealed, were it not for our celestial mirror—our reflective introspection. Yet, by daring to look, we give ourselves the gift of knowledge. By acknowledging these parts of ourselves, we add new stars to our personal galaxy, expanding our self-awareness, and propelling our growth.

Remember, North Star Seeker, a universe doesn't shy away from its black holes, and neither should we. Black holes, while intimidating, are an essential component of the cosmic landscape. They force us to face our fears, to confront our limitations. And in doing so, they give us an opportunity to grow stronger, braver, wiser.

The celestial mirror, this tool of introspection, gives us the power to explore the uncharted territories of our soul. By courageously delving into the hidden recesses of our psyche, we get to know our true selves. We unearth potential that we may not have known we possessed, we face fears that we may not have had the courage to acknowledge before, and we foster growth that we may not have thought possible.

Just as a telescope needs to be adjusted to observe different parts of the spectrum, so too must our perspective be adjusted to see the various parts of ourselves. There might be parts of us that we are not proud of, traits or past actions that we might prefer to keep hidden in the darkness. But remember, every star in the sky, every distant galaxy, and every mysterious black hole, no matter how faint or far, contributes to the cosmic spectacle. And it's the same with you. Each element of your personality, each episode in your life story, no matter how insignificant or unflattering it may seem, contributes to the person you are.

You are not just the person you are at your best, but also the person you are at your worst. You are your joys and your sorrows, your hopes and your fears, your dreams, and your doubts. You are the full spectrum of experiences, emotions, and states of being. Embrace them all, for they are what make you unique. They are what make you a Star Seeker.

To truly reflect on self-growth, you must embrace the full spectrum of your being. This acceptance of our full selves is not a destination, but a continuous journey, just like our exploration of the vast cosmos. With every glance into your celestial mirror, dare to see your true colors, for they are the irreplaceable hues of your unique journey towards Galactic Excellence.

⟨ ⟩

The Supernova: Transformative Growth

Among the celestial events that the mirror of the cosmos reveals, perhaps none is as spectacularly transformative as the supernova. A supernova, the explosive death of a star, is an event of cataclysmic change. It is, quite literally, a stellar death leading to cosmic rebirth. The energy and elements released during a supernova enrich the interstellar medium, serving as the building blocks for new stars, new planets, and potentially, new life.

This cosmic event, in all its glorious paradox, is a potent metaphor for the transformative power of introspection in our lives.

Self-reflection may bring us to confront challenging truths about ourselves, truths that may initially feel like an internal upheaval, a detonation of our self-perception. You might feel that your well-organized understanding of yourself is falling apart, mirroring a star's end of life cycle. But just as the supernova's brilliant explosion yields elements vital for new celestial bodies, this internal disruption paves the way for transformative self-growth.

Through introspection, we can break down our outdated beliefs about ourselves, reexamine our values, question our self-imposed limitations, and challenge our biases. As we do so, we create space for new insights to emerge, for renewed understanding to blossom, and for a more authentic self-concept to take form. Our personal supernova, though initially disorienting, leads us to a clearer, deeper, and more comprehensive understanding of who we are and who we can become.

Moreover, just as a supernova contributes significantly to the surrounding universe, your transformative self-growth reverberates through your life. Your relationships may evolve as you express your more authentic self. Your approach to challenges can shift as you acknowledge and address your shadows. Your pursuit of Galactic Excellence may take on a new trajectory as you reassess your priorities.

So, North Star Seeker, when you find yourself amidst an internal supernova, remember the cosmos. Feel the turmoil, endure the disintegration, and embrace the chaos, for it is the precursor to a splendid rebirth. Trust in the process and know that just as a supernova paves the way for a celestial renewal, your internal upheaval is a path to profound personal transformation.

Keep reflecting, keep evolving, and keep seeking. For the path to Galactic Excellence lies not just among the stars but also within you. And with each reflection, you step closer to your destiny. Your journey continues, one reflection at a time.

Chapter 12: Crossing the Event Horizon - Beyond the Comfort Zone

The Event Horizon - Boundary of the Known

Imagine standing at the edge of the universe, staring at a colossal black hole, its gaping mouth threatening to swallow anything that dares to venture too close. It radiates an ominous yet enchanting aura of mystery, its center cloaked in a veil of uncertainty. This is the event horizon, the precipice where the known universe ends and an enigmatic realm begins.

Just as we gaze into the depths of a black hole with an intoxicating mix of fear and fascination, we all have our own personal event horizons. They are not made of cosmic dust or interstellar gas, but of experiences, emotions, and habits that cocoon us in a warm, familiar comfort zone.

But what lies beyond that comfort zone? What untold mysteries and possibilities lay waiting, just beyond the event horizon of our everyday routines?

Just as a black hole is a fundamental part of our cosmos, the boundaries of our comfort zone are integral to our lives. They serve to keep us safe and stable, providing a comforting orbit within the vast universe of experiences. But to truly grow—to explore, to discover, to change—we must venture past these boundaries.

Remember, every star seeker must cross the event horizon to reach Galactic Excellence. It's time to prepare for that exciting journey. Let's step beyond the known, and embrace the beauty of the mysterious, for the path to true growth lies just beyond our comfort zones. It's time to cross your event horizon.

《 》

Understanding Your Comfort Zone: The Safe Orbit

Identifying your event horizon starts with noticing areas of distortion—the moments when your heartbeat quickens, your mind races, or your palms get sweaty. It's that presentation you've been avoiding because public speaking makes you nervous. It's that difficult conversation you've been postponing because you fear the outcome. It's that project you've been hesitant to take on because it demands skills you have yet to master.

Your event horizon lies where your comfort zone ends and your learning zone begins. It's the boundary of your current abilities, the edge of what you believe is possible. But, unlike the event horizon of a black hole, crossing this boundary won't lead to destruction—it leads to transformation.

Recognizing your event horizon is the first step in learning how to navigate it. When you're aware of your limits, you can work towards expanding them. Remember, every person you admire for their Galactic Excellence—their skill, their success, their courage—has crossed their event horizon time and again, turning the unknown into the known, the uncomfortable into the familiar.

Our event horizons call to us, inviting us to explore what lies beyond. But crossing this threshold requires courage, curiosity, and a commitment to growth.

《 》

Singularity and Transformation: The Power of Uncomfortable

Once we've taken that leap of faith and crossed the event horizon of our comfort zone, we plunge towards a unique point—a singularity in our personal universe. Just as a black hole conceals a singularity at its heart, a point of infinite density and gravitational pull, our venture beyond the comfort zone leads us to a singular point of transformation. It's an experience marked by intensity and profound growth, and its power lies in its ability to unsettle and provoke us into evolving.

The singularity of a black hole is a realm where our understanding of physics warps and conventional rules no longer apply. Similarly, when we venture beyond the event horizon of our comfort zone, we enter a space where our usual routines and thought patterns are disrupted, where we must devise new ways of thinking and acting. This is the essence of the singularity of discomfort—it propels us out of our habitual modes and compels us to innovate, to adapt, and ultimately, to evolve.

The process can be overwhelming and even distressing. When we're thrown into situations that stretch our abilities, we may stumble, we may fall, we may even feel like retreating. But it's in these trials that we find our true grit. Like a cosmic forge, the singularity of discomfort molds and shapes us, refining our skills, building our resilience, and kindling our inner fire. This pressure, intense as it may be, works to fashion us into more refined, capable, and resilient versions of ourselves.

It's crucial, however, to remember that the power of uncomfortable doesn't mean we need to seek out hardship for the sake of it. Rather, it's about understanding that growth and comfort rarely ride the same vehicle. It's about consciously choosing to step into challenges that serve our growth, choosing to see discomfort as a crucible for transformation rather than a pitfall to be avoided.

In this way, the power of uncomfortable echoes the transformative potential at the heart of a black hole. Though cloaked in mystery and fraught with danger, it promises profound growth and transformation for those who dare to journey into its depths. As you navigate the singularity of your personal discomfort, remember that this is your moment of transformation, your moment to morph into the stellar entity you are destined to become. Embrace the power of uncomfortable, Star Seeker, and let it propel you towards the dazzling heights of your Galactic Excellence.

《 》

Navigating the Unknown: Strategies for Exploring Beyond

Stepping outside the familiarity of our comfort zone is akin to venturing into uncharted space—thrilling, yet equally daunting. As North Star Seekers, it's our mission to go beyond the horizon and explore the untrodden terrains of personal and professional growth. This exploration, however, calls for a reliable compass and effective strategies that guide our steps in the vast, nebulous realm of the unknown.

Step 1: **Cultivate Curiosity**

Just as an astronomer gazes at the cosmos with curiosity, foster a sense of intrigue and openness towards the unknown. Embrace the idea that every encounter with something unfamiliar is an opportunity for learning and growth. Curiosity can light up the darkest corners of uncertainty, turning fear into fascination, doubt into discovery.

Step 2: **Build a Support System**

On this solitary journey into the uncharted territories, it's vital to have a robust support system. Like the ground control team in a space mission, these are the people who provide guidance, encouragement, and reinforcement when things get tough. Seek mentors who can share their experiences, friends who radiate positivity, and a community that uplifts your spirits.

Step 3: Set Incremental Goals

Breaking the journey down into smaller, manageable goals can make the unknown seem less daunting. Think of it like mapping out a journey across the cosmos—one star at a time. Each small goal achieved brings you closer to your Galactic Excellence, transforming the immense void of the unknown into a navigable constellation of achievements.

Step 4: Embrace Failure as a Teacher

Just as black holes, those celestial phenomena we often associate with destruction, are essential for galaxy formation, failures are crucial for your personal evolution. Each misstep is an opportunity to learn, to improve, and to grow. As the saying goes, there are no failures, only lessons.

Step 5: Practice Self-Care

Finally, remember to take care of yourself on this demanding journey. Just as astronauts need to maintain their physical and mental health during a space mission, Star Seekers also need to ensure their well-being. Regular rest, healthy eating, physical exercise, and mindfulness are not just essential for survival, but they are the fuel that propels you further into the unknown.

Remember, the greatest secrets of the universe aren't found in the safety of known galaxies, but in the mysterious realms beyond. So, embrace the adventure and plunge into the voyage of a lifetime.

Chapter 13: Supernova Creativity - The Big Bang of Ideas

Supernova Creativity - Igniting the Cosmic Spark

Every second, somewhere in the vast expanses of the universe, a star exhausts its nuclear fuel and collapses under its own gravity, igniting a spectacular explosion - a supernova. This grand cosmic event is not simply the death of a star but a rebirth, a catalyst for the creation of new stars, planets, and potentially, life itself. The sheer intensity of the explosion enriches the universe with heavier elements, setting the stage for the miracle of creation to unfold anew.

In many ways, our creativity mirrors this awe-inspiring celestial process. Just like a supernova, each creative idea that we conceive and execute has the potential to dramatically enrich our world, ushering in new paradigms, solutions, and ways of thinking. The spark of creativity within us can serve as a potent force, not merely for personal fulfillment but for the evolution of our societies and civilizations.

This chapter is dedicated to celebrating this 'Supernova Creativity'. We will delve into the understanding of what creativity is, how it works, and how we can nurture it. The parallels drawn from the life of a star to the journey of a creative thought will serve as a backdrop, providing an imaginative and motivating way to comprehend this process.

We, as North Star Seekers, are not just passive observers of the celestial spectacle but active participants in this cosmic dance of creation. Let's ignite the cosmic spark within us and embark on this exciting exploration of Supernova Creativity. Let this be the big bang that lights up the universe of your ideas and imagination.

⟨ ⟩

Understanding Creativity: The Star Within

Every star in the night sky is a powerful fusion reactor, constantly converting hydrogen into helium, in the process releasing enormous amounts of energy that light up the cosmos. And just like these stars, each of us possesses an inner core of creativity that holds the potential to illuminate not just our lives but also the lives of those around us.

But what exactly is creativity?

At its simplest, creativity is the ability to generate new, original ideas, solutions, or artistic expressions that are valuable in some way. However, it is more than just a mental process. Creativity is also an expression of our unique perspectives, experiences, and imaginations. It represents the embodiment of our individuality, and it's through creativity that we leave our indelible fingerprints on the canvas of time.

The power of creativity is multifaceted. It can solve complex problems, fuel innovation, inspire art, shape societies, and drive the evolution of human thought. Just as a star gives warmth, light, and life, so does creativity nourish our intellect, enrich our experiences, and breathe life into our dreams and aspirations.

Recognizing the creativity within us is akin to acknowledging the existence of an inner star – a cosmic entity of immense potential. Just as a star derives its energy from its core, our creative power lies at the very essence of who we are. It's ever-present, constantly fusing experiences and knowledge to create something new and radiant.

Let's turn our telescopes inward and seek the star within. Let's tap into the nuclear fusion of our minds, where ideas meet and meld, giving birth to new concepts and perspectives. As we journey towards Galactic Excellence, let's harness the energy of our inner stars, light up the sky with our ideas, and illuminate the universe with our creativity.

《 》

Barriers to Creativity: Gravity Wells and Black Holes

In our galactic journey towards creative supernova, we may encounter cosmic phenomena that seem to hinder our progress - gravity wells and black holes. Just as these celestial bodies can distort the path of light, certain obstacles can distort our creative paths, making the journey towards the realization of our ideas more challenging. However, like seasoned space explorers, we must learn to navigate these hazards. Let's delve into some of these barriers to creativity and how to maneuver around them.

1. **Gravity Wells**: Fear and Self-Doubt

The gravity well, a distortion in the fabric of space-time around a massive object, represents the fear and self-doubt that can pull us away from our creative journey. We may fear rejection, ridicule, or failure, and these fears can be strong enough to pull us off course, much like a gravity well can divert a spacecraft's trajectory.

To navigate these wells of fear and self-doubt, we must remember that every Star Seeker has these moments of insecurity. Allow yourself the grace of being imperfect. Remember that failure is a natural part of the creative process, not a sign of weakness. Don't let the gravity well of fear pull you off course. Break free from its pull with the rocket fuel of self-belief and resilience.

2. **Black Holes**: Overthinking and Perfectionism

Black holes, with their immense gravitational pull from which nothing, not even light, can escape, represent the trap of overthinking and perfectionism. We may spend so much time fine-tuning an idea that we never move past the conception stage, stuck in a black hole of constant revision and hesitation.

Escaping this black hole requires a leap of faith. Realize that an idea doesn't have to be perfect to be brilliant. Sometimes the beauty lies in the imperfections, in the raw and genuine creativity. The first step towards overcoming, overthinking, and perfectionism is to trust in the value of your ideas, and to allow them to see the light of day, imperfect as they might be.

《 》

The Supernova Moment: Unleashing Creative Potential

The Supernova Moment is the exact instance when an idea or a concept that has been slowly forming within the nebula of your mind, suddenly and dramatically bursts forth, illuminating your understanding and vision. This could be the groundbreaking solution to a long-standing problem, a revolutionary idea that disrupts the norm, or a moment of profound realization that reshapes your perspective.

Just like the conditions within a star that lead to a supernova, there are conditions within our minds that make these Supernova Moments possible. Let's explore how we can cultivate these conditions.

1. Feed Your Mind

The energy within a star that ultimately powers a supernova comes from its fusion reactions. Similarly, your mind's energy comes from a continuous intake of information, experiences, and ideas. Feed your mind a rich and diverse diet of knowledge and experiences. Read widely, travel, engage in new activities, meet different people. This wealth of input serves as the fuel that powers the fusion of ideas within your mind.

2. Embrace the Process

Just as a star takes millions of years to reach its supernova stage, your creative process requires patience. The incubation of an idea can take time, and that's okay. Creativity is not a sprint; it's a marathon. Embrace the journey, and understand that each step you take, no matter how small it may seem, is a step closer to your Supernova Moment.

3. Create Space for Creativity

A star needs space to explode into a supernova. In the same vein, creativity needs room to bloom. Make space for creativity in your daily routine. Dedicate time to brainstorming, daydreaming, and exploring your thoughts. This is when the sparks fly and the likelihood of reaching a Supernova Moment skyrockets.

4. Courage to Ignite

Finally, a supernova occurs when a star has the courage to let go, to explode, to transform. Similarly, the courage to embrace your ideas, to share them, and to allow them to transform you and the world around you is critical. Fear not the magnitude of your ideas. Embrace them, ignite them, and let them light up your path to Galactic Excellence.

Remember, North Star Seeker, the cosmos within your minds is teeming with unexplored ideas and unignited creative energy, awaiting its Supernova Moment. Cultivate the conditions for it, and when it comes, embrace it with all the awe and wonder it deserves. Because your Supernova Moment could be the Big Bang of ideas that reshapes your world.

〈 〉

Creativity as a Force for Change: Cosmic Rays of Innovation

On a societal level, creativity can be a catalyst for significant change. It is the engine that drives social, political, and cultural evolution. It can break down barriers, challenge traditional norms, and enable us to imagine a more equitable and harmonious world. Think about the societal supernovas who changed the course of history through their creative thinking, people like Martin Luther King Jr., Marie Curie, or Mahatma Gandhi. They were the cosmic rays whose innovative ideas traversed the cosmos of human society, triggering reactions that still reverberate today.

And in the workplace, creativity is the cornerstone of innovation. It helps businesses stay competitive, fosters a positive work environment, and promotes a culture of continual learning and improvement. It allows us to dream big, take risks, and turn our ambitious visions into reality. Every significant breakthrough, every disruptive technology, every revolutionary product was once a spark of creativity in someone's mind.

So, North Star Seeker, remember to harness your creativity, to channel your Cosmic Rays of Innovation. Let it shine in your personal life, let it resonate in your society, let it revolutionize your workplace. Just as a supernova enriches the cosmos with its creative energy, so too can you enrich your world with the explosive potential of your creativity. In this way, we can all contribute to the grand tapestry of galactic progress, each a star in the constellation of change.

The human spirit thrives on connection and our creativity is no exception. As social beings, we are wired to collaborate, to share ideas, to inspire and be inspired. When we harness this innate propensity towards collaboration, we unlock a wellspring of collective creativity. A creativity that is richer, deeper, and more multifaceted than what we could ever achieve alone.

Collective creativity, much like a constellation, begins with a shared vision. It is this vision that guides the collective towards a common purpose. It acts as the north star, providing a sense of direction and a guiding light in the creative journey. However, having a shared vision does not mean uniformity of thought. On the contrary, it thrives on diversity, just as a constellation is composed of stars of varying sizes, brightness, and colors.

Embrace diversity of thought, experiences, and skills. Each member of the team brings a unique set of perspectives to the table and it is this very uniqueness that enriches the collective creative output. Encourage open dialogue and a free exchange of ideas, just as stars in a constellation shine brightly in their individual capacities while contributing to the overall pattern.

Chapter 14: Navigating the Spiral Galaxy - Embracing Continual Evolution

Obstacles to Evolution: Galactic Collisions and Cosmic Clouds

In our vast universe, galaxies gracefully spin their way through the cosmic expanse, but they too encounter obstacles. They face collisions with other galaxies, get shrouded in cosmic clouds, or find their paths altered by the mysterious pull of dark matter. These galactic events serve as fitting metaphors for the hurdles we face in our personal journey towards continual evolution.

Just as galaxies might face collisions, so too do we encounter conflicts in our lives. These can come in many forms—differences of opinion, personal or professional disagreements, or even internal conflicts where our beliefs and values might clash with our circumstances or actions. Such collisions can feel disruptive, chaotic, even damaging. Yet, much like the resulting merger of galaxies can give birth to new stars, our collisions also hold transformative potential. Conflicts challenge our perspectives, push us to think critically and provide an opportunity to grow and learn from our experiences.

Cosmic clouds—nebulae of dust and gas—can obscure the view of a galaxy, just as doubt, fear, or lack of self-confidence can cloud our path to continual evolution. These barriers can make us lose sight of our goals, our visions, and even our identity. But remember, it's within these very nebulae that new stars are born. So, when we find ourselves clouded by fear or doubt, let's remind ourselves that it's often in these cloudy, uncertain periods that we find the raw materials for personal growth.

Just as the invisible dark matter can alter a galaxy's path, unseen external influences in our lives—societal pressures, expectations from others, unforeseen circumstances—can sometimes divert us from our chosen path. These influences, though invisible, are strong, but they need not dictate our journey. By becoming aware of these external pulls, we can learn to navigate their influence, keeping true to our own path and maintaining our orbit.

Navigating the spiral galaxy of life isn't an easy task—it's a challenging, unending journey of twists and turns. There will be moments of clarity and times of obscurity, periods of peace and instances of collision. Yet, with each revolution, with every challenge faced and overcome, we grow—we evolve. By learning to see obstacles as opportunities for growth, we can transform galactic collisions into new constellations, cosmic clouds into star-forming nebulae, and unseen pulls into navigational aids. In this way, we keep spiraling upward in our quest for Galactic Excellence.

《 》

Strategies for Continual Evolution: Star Seeker's Guide

As the celestial bodies above continue on their unending journey of evolution, so must we maintain an unwavering commitment to personal growth and transformation. In our quest for Galactic Excellence, we must seek strategies and tools to nurture our continual evolution, much like the nurturing cosmic forces that guide a galaxy. Herein lies the Star Seeker's Guide—a compass for your journey of unending growth.

Strategy 1: **Embrace a Growth Mindset** - Like a galaxy expanding into the universe's untapped potential, develop an open mindset that is receptive to change and hungry for growth. Believe in your ability to learn, evolve, and adapt, no matter the circumstances. See every experience, every challenge, every triumph and setback, as an opportunity for growth.

Strategy 2: **Cultivate Lifelong Learning** - Akin to a star's continuous fusion process, keep your quest for knowledge and understanding burning. Remain perpetually curious, constantly seeking to learn more, to understand deeper, to explore further. Make every day an opportunity to learn something new.

Strategy 3: **Practice Resilience** - Like a galaxy weathering the chaos of cosmic collisions, learn to withstand the trials and tribulations of life. When confronted with obstacles, don't crumble; instead, use them as fuel for your transformation.

Strategy 4: **Seek and Implement Feedback** - Just as celestial bodies guide their trajectories using gravitational feedback, seek and implement constructive criticism to improve and evolve. See feedback not as a critique of your current state, but as a guide to becoming a better version of yourself.

Strategy 5: **Embrace Diversity** - Just as a galaxy teems with a variety of stars, planets, and cosmic phenomena, value the richness that diverse experiences, perspectives, and people bring to your life. This diversity can offer you new ways of thinking, new ideas, and new paths towards growth and understanding.

Strategy 6: **Nurture Creativity** - Like the spontaneous birth of new stars in a galaxy, foster an environment where creativity and innovation can thrive. Explore new ways of doing things, seek unconventional solutions, and dare to think differently.

Remember, each person's path to Galactic Excellence is as unique as the galaxies dotting our night sky. There is no one-size-fits-all strategy, no universally correct course. What matters is your willingness to grow, to learn, and to adapt, guided by the twinkling stars above and the unquenchable flame of your spirit within. As a North Star Seeker, your journey towards continual evolution is yours alone—but know that the cosmos itself is with you every step of the way.

Chapter 15: Arrival: Your Own Universe - Living Your Galactic Excellence

Arrival at Your Own Universe

As your cosmic voyage draws to a close, you find yourself standing on the precipice of your own universe, a testament to the quest you undertook. You, the courageous North Star Seeker, have traversed the galaxy of personal growth and self-improvement, encountering nebulae of knowledge, hurdling over asteroids of doubt, and reaching stellar heights of accomplishment.

Now, you feel a sense of accomplishment swell within you, your heart pulsing with the rhythm of newfound wisdom. Your eyes, once gazing upwards to the stars with questions and longing, now reflect the luminescent wisdom of those celestial bodies.

Yet, this feeling of completion is not the end, Star Seeker, it is the beginning. The beginning of understanding, the genesis of transformation. You have grown not merely in knowledge but in perspective, in courage, and in empathy. The journey has changed you, altered the core of who you are and how you perceive the universe around you.

The Universe, once an intimidating expanse of the unknown, now stands as a testament to your journey, a canvas upon which your new insights and perspectives paint a richer, more vibrant picture. The sense of achievement you feel now isn't just about reaching the destination;

it's about embracing the growth, the changes, the evolution you've experienced along your voyage.

For you have not only journeyed through the cosmos; you have journeyed within yourself. You have faced the dark void of uncertainty, the swirling nebula of self-doubt, and the black holes of fear. You have emerged from them not as a mere traveler, but as an explorer of the soul and a conqueror of your fears. This is your universe, and you have learned to navigate it with the grace and fortitude of a celestial voyager.

This sense of accomplishment and realization is your first step into a larger world, the world of living in Galactic Excellence. So, come forth, Star Seeker, take your well-deserved place among the cosmos as we delve into what it truly means to live your Galactic Excellence.

《 》

Retrospective: The Journey through the Cosmos

As you stand now, the light of your own universe illuminating your path, let us embark on a journey backward through the cosmos, revisiting the radiant orbs of wisdom you collected along your path to Galactic Excellence.

Remember the departure from your Earthly Limits in Chapter 1, when you dared to unchain yourself from the terrestrial bounds of self-doubt and fear, launching yourself into the expansive universe of potential. You embraced the infinity of possibility, standing at the precipice of the unknown and taking the first brave leap into the star-studded void.

In Chapter 2, you faced the Black Hole of Fear, staring down the gnashing maw of your deepest anxieties and uncertainties. Yet, instead of succumbing, you found the courage within you to continue, armed with tools and strategies to navigate the gravitational pull from that which you were afraid of.

Through the Starlight of Self-Reflection in Chapter 3, you turned your gaze inward, unearthing the insights buried within the stardust of your being. You learned to see yourself not as a mere speck in the universe, but as a star in your own right with your unique light to offer to the cosmos.

The Interstellar Communication in Chapter 4 provided you with a cosmic perspective on connecting with others. It shed light on the importance of empathetic and open communication, akin to the celestial bodies communicating across light-years with their luminous signals.

On the Comet of Change in Chapter 5, you grappled with the speed of transformation, learning that change is a constant companion on the journey towards Galactic Excellence. The ability to adapt and evolve is part of your universal journey, a comet that propels you towards your goals.

From the Supernova Creativity in Chapter 13, you learned that your ideas and innovative thinking are as powerful as a supernova's burst, altering the universe around them with their explosive impact. You embraced the beauty and importance of your own creative power.

And finally, in Chapter 14, Navigating the Spiral Galaxy, you learned the significance of continual evolution and lifelong learning. Like a galaxy, you are ever-evolving, continually growing and changing, never static.

Reflect on these core insights and recognize the transformative journey you've embarked on. Each chapter, a celestial body you visited, left you with newfound knowledge, perspectives, and tools to navigate the cosmos of your potential. Now, you are more than just a Star Seeker; you are a voyager, a cosmic pioneer who has carved a path through the universe of self-growth and self-improvement. But remember, the voyage doesn't end here. The journey continues ever spiraling towards the infinity of Galactic Excellence.

⟨ ⟩

Living Your Galactic Excellence: From Star Seeker to Star Shaper

The path to excellence is not a linear voyage, but a continuous spiral, much like the whirling arms of our Milky Way. Throughout this journey, you have transformed from a Star Seeker to a Star Shaper. This is no minor transition, but rather a cosmic shift in identity. So, what does it mean to be a Star Shaper? And how can you live your Galactic Excellence in everyday life?

Being a **Star Shaper** means being an architect of your own universe, a cosmic gardener tending to your galaxy of potential. It involves understanding that each of us is a unique amalgamation of stardust and spirit, with a unique light to shine on the universe. Your Galactic Excellence is the beacon that lights your path, your guide in the everlasting voyage of growth and self-discovery.

To live your Galactic Excellence is to live a life of purpose, of continual exploration, learning, and growth. It's to embrace change as a comet that propels you forward, to understand that obstacles and black holes are opportunities for transformation.

But how do you integrate this into the mundane terrestrial reality? Start by creating a cosmic landscape in your everyday life. Curate an environment that nurtures your creativity, encourages innovation, and stimulates growth. Cultivate relationships that fuel your voyage, connecting with others in a way that promotes mutual understanding and respect.

Embrace the philosophy of the Spiral Galaxy Principle. Keep learning, keep evolving, and keep adapting. Your thirst for knowledge and understanding should be as insatiable as a black hole, pulling in information and experiences that enrich your universe.

Also, reflect regularly on your journey, using self-reflection to understand your strengths and identify areas for growth. Remember, introspection is the telescope that lets you observe the far reaches of your inner cosmos.

And finally, radiate your Galactic Excellence outward. Share your unique light with the world, contributing your talents, ideas, and energy to make a positive impact. As a Star Shaper, you don't just exist in the universe - you shape it, mold it, and illuminate it.

Star Shaper, this is your new identity, a mantle of galactic responsibility, and an insignia of honor. Wear it with pride and live your Galactic Excellence in every step of your journey, from the terrestrial to the cosmic, and in every corner of your universe. As you continue your voyage, **remember**: You are not just navigating the cosmos; you are now a part of its grand evolution.

$$\langle\!\langle \ \rangle\!\rangle$$

Universal Alignment: The Power of the Principles

The principles we've explored together are not just abstract concepts floating in the ether of thought, but practical tools for shaping the vast universe of your life. They are the cosmic forces propelling your journey from Star Seeker to Star Shaper. These principles—The Nebula of Potential, The Supernova Creativity, The Spiral Galaxy Principle—are no mere metaphors, but dynamic codes of living that align your life with the rhythms of the universe.

The Power of the Principles lies in their ability to guide your voyage, allowing you to navigate the cosmos of your life with wisdom and confidence. Like cosmic coordinates, they give direction to your journey, guiding your path as you spiral towards your own Galactic Excellence.

The Nebula of Potential is a reminder that within you lies an unfathomable reservoir of talent, passion, and strength waiting to be ignited. It inspires you to delve into the depths of your potential and encourages you to give shape to the nebulous dreams and ideas swirling within your being.

Supernova Creativity speaks to the explosive power of your imagination, the ability to birth brilliance from the depths of your mind. It invites you to cultivate conditions that trigger those bursts of insight, those moments when a world of possibilities open before your eyes.

The Spiral Galaxy Principle, meanwhile, instills in you the spirit of endless evolution, urging you to embrace the unceasing spiral of learning, growth, and change. It encourages you to view your journey not as a straight path but as a spiral, where each revolution brings you closer to your unique Galactic Excellence.

Living in alignment with these principles is like tuning your personal frequency to the harmonic resonance of the cosmos. It aligns your actions, decisions, and experiences with the fundamental rhythms of the universe, ensuring that you're not just a passive voyager but an active shaper of your destiny.

Remember, Star Shaper, your universe is not something external to you—it exists within you. Every thought, every action, every decision is a gravitational wave that ripples through your universe, shaping the galaxies of your life. Align yourself with these principles, let them be your guiding stars, and you'll not just find your way in the universe—you'll create your own way, one star at a time.

《 》

Practical Galaxy: Tools and Strategies for Galactic Living

As we step into the realm of Galactic Living, the nebulous concepts we've explored begin to take concrete form. The challenge—and the joy—of this phase of the journey is to integrate these principles into the rhythm of your everyday life, turning the abstract into the actionable, the cosmic into the commonplace.

In your hand, you now hold the cosmic compass, the tools and strategies to navigate your universe towards Galactic Excellence. Let's examine them together, casting starlight upon each to illuminate their power and potential in your life.

Your Nebulous Notebook: Similar to the journaling we explored in earlier chapters, maintain a 'Nebulous Notebook'. Fill it with thoughts, ideas, dreams, and goals—big or small. It's a place for capturing your nebula of potential and giving it form. Regularly review your entries to see how your ideas develop, evolve, and take shape over time.

The Supernova Spark: Set aside a dedicated 'creative time' each day. It can be fifteen minutes or an hour—the duration is less important than the regularity. Use this time to brainstorm, sketch, write, or simply allow your mind to wander. This practice cultivates conditions for your Supernova Creativity, your explosive moments of innovation and insight.

The Spiral Staircase: Create a learning plan that reflects your Spiral Galaxy Principle. Choose topics or skills that excite you and pursue them with curiosity. Each step you take on this staircase is a step towards your Galactic Excellence. Remember, every subject you explore, every skill you develop, is a revolution in your spiral of learning.

Stargazing for Success: Practice mindful reflection at the end of each day. Consider the lessons learned, challenges faced, and victories won. This daily practice of 'stargazing' helps you align your actions with your principles and allows you to learn from your experiences.

These tools and strategies aren't mere assignments; they're celestial instruments for your journey. With these in hand, you're no longer a Star Seeker—you're a Star Shaper, shaping the cosmic course of your life.

As you step forward in your voyage, **remember**: Galactic Excellence is not a destination but a way of journeying. It's about continual evolution, embracing change, and striving for lifelong learning. It's about awakening to your potential, sparking your creativity, and shaping your destiny.

Keep these tools close, Star Shaper, and let them guide you as you journey onward, spiraling ever closer towards your Galactic Excellence.

⟨ ⟩

E ternal Voyage: The Journey Never Ends

When we set out on this cosmic journey together, we marked a beginning. You, the valiant Star Seeker, were preparing for a grand quest, your sights set on the dazzling possibilities that awaited. Now, standing at the pinnacle of this chapter, looking back at the galaxies traversed, you may wonder: Have we arrived? Is this the end of our journey?

Star Shaper, in truth, this is not the end, but another beginning. For our voyage towards Galactic Excellence is not marked by an arrival point, but by the journey itself. It is an ongoing expedition through the cosmos of self-improvement, a pilgrimage to the furthest reaches of your potential. The journey, with its spiral paths and nebula of ideas, supernova sparks and black hole breakthroughs, is the destination.

Every step you take, every change you make, every spark of creativity you ignite, each contributes to the cosmic dance of growth and evolution. And so, your journey continues, like the stars that journey across the cosmos, ever moving, ever shining, even when they seem to be at rest.

Remember, the essence of Galactic Excellence lies in embracing the journey as an endless exploration of your universe. Each new day brings with it an opportunity for a fresh start, a new revolution on your spiral path, a chance to ignite a supernova of creativity. It's in these daily moments of striving and growth, of curiosity and exploration, that you truly live your Galactic Excellence.

As you venture forward into the uncharted territories of your universe, remember the power that resides within you—the power to shape, to evolve, and to illuminate. As a Star Shaper, you carry the light of galaxies within you, a light that can pierce the darkest cosmic clouds, guiding you along your spiral path.

And so, Star Shaper, you realize: the journey towards Galactic Excellence doesn't end. It only deepens, spiraling further into the cosmos of potential. It is a voyage without a final port, a song without a closing note, a story without an ending. And you are its author, its composer, its captain.

The voyage of Galactic Excellence, your voyage, is eternal, boundless as the cosmos itself. And that is a journey worth undertaking. So, let us journey on, for the cosmos awaits, and your story is far from over. It's a grand, eternal voyage, and it continues with the breaking of each new dawn.

《 》

Cosmic Connection: Being a Part of the Greater Universe

As you, Star Shaper, embark on your eternal voyage, you may feel small amidst the cosmic expanse of potential. You might gaze upon the glittering galaxies and wonder, "Where do I fit into this grand scheme?"

Remember, you are not a lone traveler adrift in the cosmic ocean. Instead, you are an integral part of the vast and mesmerizing tapestry of existence. Your journey towards Galactic Excellence does not exist in isolation but is part of the harmonic symphony of the cosmos.

Consider this: when you grow, you do not grow alone. Your growth influences those around you. A spark of your creativity may ignite a supernova in someone else. Your journey through the spiral galaxy of continual evolution may guide others on their path. Your pursuit of Galactic Excellence has ripples, sending waves across the cosmic ocean, touching distant shores you may never see.

This understanding underscores a profound truth: in your quest for Galactic Excellence, you are not merely shaping your universe—you are contributing to the harmony of the broader universe.

Every thread matters. Your thread—vibrant, unique, and irreplaceable—adds a distinct color, texture, and pattern. It weaves its way through the fabric of existence, knotting itself with other threads, creating an intricate, interconnected pattern of life, growth, and Galactic Excellence. You are not just a tiny speck in the universe; you are the universe experiencing itself. Through your voyage, you're not only seeking stars, you're creating them, shaping them.

The universe is your canvas. You, **Star Shaper**, are the artist. So, step forth and paint your masterpiece with the brushstrokes of Galactic Excellence. Your cosmic voyage awaits!

Don't miss out!

Visit the website below and you can sign up to receive emails whenever Cj TruHeart publishes a new book. There's no charge and no obligation.

https://books2read.com/r/B-A-DIPZ-LFFMC

BOOKS 2 READ

Connecting independent readers to independent writers.

Did you love *Star Seeker: Your Mission for Galactic Excellence*? Then you should read *Game On: Your Quest for Competitive Excellence*[1] by Cj TruHeart!

Game On: Your Quest for Competitive Excellence

Unlock the game of life with lessons from the world's greatest arena: competition.

In today's rapidly evolving world, teenagers face challenges reminiscent of the most gripping video games. Pressing start on this thrilling journey, Game On: Your Quest for Competitive Excellence takes readers on an exhilarating expedition that blends the tenacity of athletic competition with the strategy and grit of gaming. Designed to resonate with the modern teenager and their guardians, this book is your manual to conquering the game of life.

---

1. https://books2read.com/u/m0oY2W

2. https://books2read.com/u/m0oY2W

Do you recall the joy of conquering a challenging level in a game, the adrenaline of scoring the winning point, or the thrill of unlocking a particularly tough achievement? Now, imagine applying that same passion, focus, and determination to real-world challenges. Whether it's acing that math exam, making the basketball team, or navigating the complexities of teenage relationships, this guidebook offers tools to transform obstacles into opportunities.

Dive into the Metaphors of Gaming and Sports: Discover how the world of competitive sports and video games intertwines with life's quests. Every setback, every victory, every strategy applied in the game offers a lesson for the real world. It's not just about winning or leveling up; it's about the journey, the experiences, and the growth.

Harness Your Competitive Spirit: Game On isn't about breeding toxic competitiveness. It's about channelling that desire to win into personal development. Learn how every scrimmage, every game, every match can teach resilience, strategy, and foresight.

Explore the Meta-game: Life isn't just about what's in front of us. It's about understanding the bigger picture—the meta-game. Learn how to zoom out, gain a holistic view, and strategize for long-term success, both in competitions and in life's myriad challenges.

Personal Growth and Self-Reflection: Equipped with checkpoints and reflection breaks, this book encourages young minds to introspect, understand their strengths and weaknesses, and carve their unique path to excellence.

Building Allies and Understanding NPCs: Navigate the world of relationships, friendships, and mentorships. Just as in games, every character we interact with in real life offers a lesson, a challenge, or a helping hand.

Parents, guardians, and mentors will find in this book a bridge to connect with the younger generation. Understanding their challenges, dreams, and fears through metaphors that resonate with them can foster more empathetic and effective communication.

Empower the young adults in your life to see their challenges, not as insurmountable obstacles, but as levels awaiting mastery. Encourage them to press play on their journey of personal development, fostering a mindset that doesn't just aim for success but cherishes the journey toward competitive excellence.

Join us on this quest, embrace the game of life, and let's achieve excellence together. The game is on—are you ready?

Game On: Your Quest for Competitive Excellence inspires readers to adopt the mindset of champions and gamers alike. By understanding life as the grandest game of all, we're not only better equipped to tackle its challenges but also to cherish its beautiful, unpredictable journey. Because in the game of life, everyone has the potential to be a champion.

Read more at https://youtube.com/@TruFinity.

Also by Cj TruHeart

Excellence for Life
Game On: Your Quest for Competitive Excellence
Star Seeker: Your Mission for Galactic Excellence

Watch for more at https://youtube.com/@TruFinity.

About the Author

Cj TruHeart

Dive into the "Excellence for Life" series and embark on a transformative voyage alongside Cj TruHeart, a guide whose journey through life's tempests has forged an unbreakable spirit. A 2x Wrestling State Champion and 4x Jiu Jitsu World Champion, Cj's accomplishments on the mat reflect his undying commitment to uplift and inspire. His tireless dedication has seen him as a beacon of hope in youth wrestling and as the driving force behind United Grappling Arts, a non-profit championing the union of mental health and physical training.

His teachings, both on the mat and in his writings, stem from personal struggles and victories, drawing deeply from his experiences as a recovered alcoholic and underscoring the power of resilience and redemption. As a devoted husband, passionate author, and mentor, Cj's philosophy resonates clear: life's greatest triumphs lie not in titles, but in the hearts touched and the legacies forged.

With Cj, each page isn't just a read—it's a revelation. It's an invitation to witness the potential within, confront challenges head-on, and to relentlessly chase after your unique excellence. Embrace the journey, and let every word inspire, uplift, and transform.

Read more at https://youtube.com/@TruFinity.

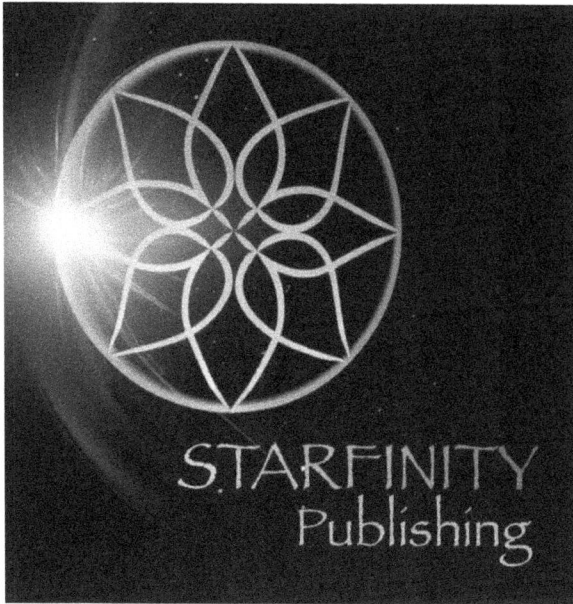

About the Publisher

Starfinity Publishing

At the heart of Starfinity Publishing lies an unwavering commitment to illuminating the pathways of excellence. With each page turned and every story unfolded, we venture beyond the ordinary, navigating the extraordinary tapestry of life's myriad challenges and triumphs. Inspired by the resilient spirit of our cornerstone author, Cj TruHeart, our catalog is a curated collection of tales and teachings that resonate deeply, touching souls and sparking transformative journeys.

Our flagship series, "Excellence for Life", encapsulates the essence of what we stand for. From the competitive fire of an athlete to the nurturing touch of a parent; from the guiding hand of a coach to the resilient heart of an individual reclaiming life from addiction's grasp – we celebrate every facet of the human experience, every endeavor toward excellence.

While the titles under our banner explore diverse terrains, from galactic adventures to the intricacies of martial arts, they share a unified message: the quest for excellence is universal, boundless, and infinitely rewarding. We believe that every individual, irrespective of age or background, has an inner star waiting to shine. Through empowering narratives, instructional insights, and heartwarming tales for children, we aim to help our readers discover, nurture, and let that inner brilliance illuminate the world around them.

But Starfinity is more than just a publishing house. We're a community. A gathering of dreamers, achievers, learners, and leaders. We are united in our pursuit of knowledge, growth, and the shared belief that stories have the power to change lives. We invite you to join our ever-expanding universe, where the limits of the sky are just the beginning.

Embark on a voyage with Starfinity Publishing. Together, let's write stories of excellence, resilience, and hope. Together, let's reach for the stars.

www.ingramcontent.com/pod-product-compliance
Lightning Source LLC
Chambersburg PA
CBHW020003290326
41935CB00007B/292